THE QURANIC SUNNAH
OF PROPHET MUHAMMAD

INTRODUCTION, TRANSLATION
AND COMPILATION BY

LALEH BAKHTIAR

LIBRARY OF ISLAM

Library of Congress Cataloging-in-Publications Data
Koran. English. *The Quranic Sunnah of Prophet Muhammad* translation and compiled by Laleh Bakhtiar.

I. Bakhtiar, Laleh. II. Title.
BP109 2006
297.1'22521-dc22 2004041455
ISBN 10: 1-56744-580-2
ISBN 13: 978-1-56744-580-0

Cover Design: 19th Century Quran cover from the Gulistan Museum, Tehran

Published by
Library of Islam

Distributed by
Kazi Publications
3023 West Belmont Avenue
Chicago IL 60618
(T) 773-267-7001; (F) 773-267-7002
email: info@kazi.org website: www.kazi.org

CONTENTS

PREFACE

Several years ago I had just completed a history of the life of Prophet Muhammad when I realized I could not send it for publication because it did not include the entire Quran, and, the entire Quran in chronological order so that it tied in with the life of the Prophet. How could I write a biography of the Prophet without including the entire Quran? I could not as it would not give the complete story of his life.[1]

I then studied the various English translations of the Quran, and in each case I found errors and methods of translation with which I could not agree. I decided that I had to translate the Quran using a different method from the usual translation process and different criteria that I believed such a translation needed in order to arrive at a translation that contained internal consistency and reliability. This took seven years. I will just present the highlights of the criteria here.[2]

Highlights of the Criteria for a Translation of the Quran.

• It should be Universal (for all of humanity) in its language.
• It should include Inclusive Language (ungrateful for *kafir*, God and not Allah).
• It should distinguish between thou, thee and thy (2nd person singular) and you and your (2nd person plural).
• It should be able to point out contradictions in previous interpretations of certain signs (verses, *ayat*) such as between 4:34 and 2:231.

In studying the Chronological Order of the Quran that I had prepared,[3] because of the criteria I had developed in the original translation, I saw another side to the Sunnah (well-trodden path, way) in the life of the Prophet. This new perspective came from the divine revelation of the Quran itself and not from the Hadith or Sira. The Quranic Sunnah is based on *sola scriptura*, by scripture alone.

The Quranic Sunnah consists of four parts:

Part 1. Quranic Signs Addressed to the Prophet Specifically (2nd person singular) in Chronological Order;
Part 2. Quranic Commands Addressed Directly to the Prophet (2nd person singular) in Chronological Order to "Say";
Part 3. Other Quranic Commands Addressed Directly to the Prophet (2nd person singular) in Chronological Order; and
Part 4. Other Quranic Commands Addressed through the Prophet to Humanity (2nd person plural) in Chronological Order.

The Quranic Sunnah of Prophet Muhammad is based on the signs revealed directly to Prophet Muhammad (2nd person singular indicated in the text as **you** or **your**) and the commands of God, the imperative form of the verbs, which are addressed directly to him (Parts 2 and 3) as well as those addressed through the Prophet to humanity at large (Part 4).

In furtherance of understanding the Quranic Sunnah, all signs (*ayat*, verses) that refer to the lives and Sunnah of other Prophets and Messengers, whose stories are revealed in the Quran, have been left out of this work. This was done so that what would remain of the Quranic signs would relate to either addressing Prophet Muhammad directly or relate directly to his prophethood.

In undertaking this work I came to an important distinction between the commands to humanity at large (the use of the 2nd person plural) as opposed to the commands related directly to Prophet Muhammad (2nd person singular). Once I realized this important distinction, I again took a look at 4:34. I found that the Quranic commands to "admonish, abandon the sleeping place and go away (*idrib, daraba*)" from wives whose resistance a husband fears address humanity at large and not the Prophet specifically. That is, the subject pronouns are you in the 2nd person plural and not the 2nd person singular. In other words, 4:34 was not directly commanded to the Prophet (2nd person singular), but to humanity at large (2nd person plural). Only a deep analysis of the Quranic Sunnah of Prophet Muhammad can help us come to further realizations and clarifications.

What will an acceptance of the Quranic Sunnah do?

There will be those who are able to take the Quranic Sunnah and what it contains as the complete Sunnah of the Prophet, as part of the divinely revealed Quran, something that God promised in the Quran that He would guard and protect. As such, it establishes the principles of the Shariah (the divine law, the way). In this case, the Shariah would be defined as: Islamic canonical law based on the teachings of the Quran, prescribing both religious and secular duties and sometimes punishments (penalties) for what is considered criminal (sinful) behavior. Thus, the Quranic Sunnah could, for some, supersede the Hadith and non-Quranic-Sunnah.

There will be others who accept the Quranic Sunnah as part of a different version of the definition of the Shariah, namely: Islamic canonical law based on the teachings of the Quran and the traditions of the Prophet (Hadith and Sunnah), prescribing both religious and secular duties and sometimes punishments (penalties) for what is considered criminal (sinful) behavior.

It should be noted, however, that Islam as a way of life (*din*) includes both belief and practice. Beliefs are the roots of this way of life (its principles, *usul al-din*) and the Shariah are the branches (*furu al-din*) of it. While the principles have their roots in the commands or imperatives in the Quran, the practices are to be found in the Hadith and other-than-Quranic Sunnah.

The question becomes: If the Shariah is based on the principles in the Quranic Sunnah, where do the practices come from? And, further: How do people know how to practice the tenets? Is there enough information in the Quranic Sunnah for the practices to be established? What differences would it make? What about the difference between Quranic commands directly to the Prophet (2nd person singular) and humanity at large (2nd person plural)? Will Muslim practices change if Muslims learn and memorize the "Say" divinely revealed commands of God to the Prophet instead of learning and memorizing the Hadith or the specialized forty Hadith series of books written over the centuries?

And: Will those Muslims who follow the Shariah based on the Quranic Sunnah be more likely to assimilate as minorities in majority non-Muslim countries? In other words, do the following of the Hadith and non-Quranic-Sunnah prevent Muslims from assimilating to their majority non-Muslim culture? Is this a good thing or a bad thing?

Introduction to the Quranic Sunnah of Prophet Muhammad

What does the word Sunnah refer to? The word, Sunnah, in a general sense, most often refers to the verbally transmitted record of the teachings, deeds, sayings and silent permissions or disapprovals of Prophet Muhammad as derived from various reports from Muhammad's companions.[3] It is also defined as a path, a way, a manner of life or well-trodden path. The Sunnah includes his specific words (*sunnah qawliyyah*), habits, practices (*sunnah al-fiiliyyah*) and silent approvals (*sunnah taqririyyah*).

The word, Sunnah, appears sixteen times in the Quran. Five of these signs refer to the way of God (*sunnat Allah*) (33:38, 33:62 where it appears twice), 40:85, 48:23 (where it appears twice), four times in reference to the way of the ancients (*sunnah al-awwalin*) and once to both *sunnat Allah* and *sunnah al-awwalin* in the same sign. (35:43)

There are many signs that command Muslims to obey God and the Messenger, which has been one of the criterion for the development of the Sunnah. There are eleven signs in which the Quran commands Muslims to: Obey God and the Messenger (3:32, 3:132); obey God and obey the Messenger (4:59, 5:92, 24:54, 47:33, 64:12); and obey God and His Messenger (8:1, 8:20, 8:46, 58:13). The twelfth sign commands Muslims: Obey the Messenger so that perhaps you will find mercy. (24:56)

Does the command to obey the Messenger not include his Quranic Sunnah? While one could say, in a sense, that the entire Quran is the Sunnah of Prophet Muhammad, as he was said to be 'the living Quran', the signs of the Quran that came to form the basis of the Shariah (the divine law) are the commands or imperatives in the Quran. These commands include the belief in the Oneness of God and the Messengership of Muhammad, the obligation to perform the formal prayer, to fast during the month of Ramadan, to give the purifying alms and to undertake the pilgrimage at least once in one's lifetime if one is able to. Known as the five pillars of Islam, these are obligatory because of God commanding them in the Quran for 'ones who submit to God'.

These commands as well as the signs that refer to the Prophet directly (2nd person singular), along with the signs that were revealed to the Prophet for all of humanity (2nd person plural) are what this work is referring to as 'the Quranic Sunnah'.

What is the Difference Between the Sunnah and the Quranic Sunnah?

The Quranic Sunnah has heretofore been left out of the sciences of the Sunnah which have been listed as including: The biography of the Prophet (*sira*), the chronicle of his battles (*al-maghazi*), his everyday sayings and acts or ways (*sunah*), his personal and moral qualities (*al-shamail*) and so forth. It is the hope that this work on the Quranic Sunnah will be listed among the sciences of the Sunnah, as well.

There are those who say that the Sunnah is not obligatory according to Islamic jurisprudence. This view clearly contradicts the Quranic Sunnah which consists of commands from God to the Prophet directly which he and his community followed.

The other-than-the-Quranic Sunnah, as understood over the centuries, was not written down during the Prophet's lifetime, but was begun to be collected at least 200 years after the death of the Prophet. The Quranic Sunnah, however, was clearly not only written down as it was revealed to the Prophet, but it was practiced by him throughout his lifetime and the community that followed him. There is nothing of doubtful authenticity or of dubious historical authenticity as is the case with some of the other Sunnah as God promises in the Quran that He will protect the Quran from being lost or changed, which, of course, includes the Quranic Sunnah, but this is not the case with the other-than-the Quran Sunnah.

The other-than-Quranic Sunnah is not as reliable as the Quranic Sunnah because the other-than-the Quranic Sunnah comes from the sayings of his Companions and those who met him and are classified as Hadith. There is no other source, other than the Quran, that Muslims can fully trust about the Sunnah of the Prophet. It is the criteria by which other Sunnah, Sira and Hadith need to be weighed.

While the Quranic Sunnah develops the criteria for all other Sunnah of Prophet Muhammad, the other-than-Quranic Sunnah is important, as previously indicated, in that it gives the details on how to pray, how to fast and so forth. This indicates that to some both are necessary. It is with the hope that an understanding of the importance of the Quranic Sunnah of Prophet Muhammad will open new fields of research and study in the life of the blessed Prophet.

About This Work

God has blessed Prophet Muhammad by revealing the Quran to him through the Angel Gabriel. The Quran (The Recitation) is considered by many to be Prophet Muhammad's greatest miracle. By presenting the signs (*ayat*) that refer directly to the Prophet, we discover the God-given Quranic Sunnah as it relates to him. This, then, takes precedence over the traditional biographies of the Prophet (*sira*) and/or Hadith (collection of traditions containing sayings of the Prophet) or Sunnah (accounts of his daily practice), and, of course, Hadith that contradict these Quranic signs.

This work is to help those who wish to study the life of Prophet Muhammad's Quranic Sunnah with a new approach that may answer questions such as: Does this approach teach us new details of the life of Prophet Muhammad that have heretofore remained unknown? Are there lessons to be learned for the Quranic method of interaction with customs practiced by non-Muslim majority societies?

An example would be learning from the commands that God gave which served as the basis for the development of Islamic jurisprudence and the Shariah. Take, for instance, his method of preserving the form or container of a custom while changing the contents. By carrying out the commands of God to him, God taught Prophet Muhammad through the Quranic revelation:

> . . . to preserve the form, the container of a custom or idea which had deep roots in society, one which people had gotten used to from generation to generation and one which was practiced in a natural manner, but he changed the contents, the spirit, the direction and the practical application of customs in a revolutionary, decisive and immediate manner.
>
> He was inspired by a particular method that he used in social combat. Without producing negative results, without containing any of the weak points of the other methods, his method contained the positive characteristics of the others. Through the customs of society that apply the brakes, he quickly attained his social goals. His revolutionary method was this: He maintained the container of a social tradition, but changed the contents.
>
> He used this method in reconciling social phenomena. He adopted a process and method that is a model for all problem solving. This method can be applied to two problems or two phenomena that in no way resemble each other. Recognizing how important this method is, we cannot fully explore it here. We can only clarify it by a few examples.
>
> Before Islam, there was a custom of total ablution that was both a belief and a superstition. The pre-Islamic Arabs believed that when a person had sexual intercourse, he or she incarnated jinn (spirits which inhabit the earth), thereby rendering both body and soul un-

clean. Until he or she found water and performed a total ablution, the jinn could not be exorcised.

Another example is the pilgrimage to Makkah. Before Islam, it was an Arab custom, full of superstitious ancestor worship. It was a glorified type of idol worship, holding economic advantage for the Quraysh tribe whereby the Kabah was filled with idols that were worshiped by the people. It had gradually come to assume this form from the time of Abraham. The Prophet was commanded to keep the form of the pre-Islamic custom of pilgrimage, as Abraham, the Friend of God, had built the Kabah for the worship of the One God, but through God's guidance, he changed the content. Now the pilgrimage was practiced to worship the One God.

The basis of the pilgrimage had been twofold: To protect the economic interests of the Quraysh merchants in Makkah and to create an artificial need among the Arab tribes for the Quraysh nobility. It was revealed to the Prophet of Islam to take this form and change it into a most beautiful and deep rite founded upon the unity of God and the oneness of humanity.

The Prophet, with his revolutionary stand, took the pilgrimage of the idol-worshipping tribes and changed it into a completely opposite rite. It was a revolutionary leap. As a result, while the Quraysh leaders opposed him because of their concern that they would lose their means of income, the Arab people underwent no anguish, no loss of values or beliefs, but rather, revived the truth and cleansed an ancient custom. They moved easily from idol worship to unity. Suddenly, they had left the past. Their society was not aware that the foundations of idol worship had been torn down. This leap, this revolutionary social method found within the [Quranic Sunnah] of the Prophet preserved the outer form, but changed its content. It maintained the container as a permanent element but changed and transformed the content. The Prophet, through the inspired method of his work, showed us that if we understand and can put his method into action, we can behave in a most enlightened and correct way.

A clear-visioned intellectual, confronted by outdated customs, ancient traditions, a dead culture and a stagnant religious and social order, takes up the mandate of the Prophet rather than submit to prejudices from the past. By this method one can reach revolutionary goals without the danger of revolution, on one hand, and without opposing the basis of faith and ancient social values on the other. By doing so, one does not remove oneself from people, nor does one become a stranger on whom people may turn and condemn. This method works because the Prophet received knowledge from the divine Infinite, because he asked for the help of revelation and because he made use of what he received.[4]

The Quranic Sunnah follows this method established by the Prophet. It takes the form of the Sunnah and changes the way that Muslims in the past have understood the content as it establishes new criteria by which to understand the life of the blessed Prophet and the humanity that he addressed.

Laleh Bakhtiar, Ph.D.
Chicago, 2015

Notes to the Preface

1. While the one volume biographies of the Prophet available in the market today are good, they do not and cannot (due to publishing restraints) tell the whole story of his life.

2. For further understanding, read the Introduction to the Sublime Quran, available for free download on www.kazi.org.

2. See bibliography: *The Chronological Quran as Revealed to Prophet Muhammad..*

3. Khaled Abou El Fadl, "What is Sharia?" March 22, 2011.

4. Ali Shariati, *Shariati on Shariati*, p 104-105.

Introduction to the Quranic Sunnah of Prophet Muhammad

Part 1. Quranic Signs Addressed to the Prophet Specifically (2nd person singular) in Chronological Order

The following signs, in the chronological order of the revelation are among the blessings that are given directly to the Prophet in the Arabic language when it refers to him either by his name, Muhammad, or Prophet or Messenger, or by the second person singular (thou, thee, thy). Thou, thee and thy are translated as "**you**" (thou, thee or "**your**," thy) in this text according to common English usage today. Note: There are also times when the Quran uses these pronouns in a general sense, referring to all of humanity and not specifically in reference to Prophet Muhammad. This is clear from the context.

Makkah Chapters

1. Chapter 96: The Blood Clot (al-Alaq)

96:1 Recite (Muhammad) in the Name of **your** Lord Who created.

96:3 Recite (Muhammad): **Your** Lord is the Most Generous.

96:8 Truly, to **your** Lord (Muhammad) is the returning.

> The Prophet receives the command: Recite the Quran in the Name of **your** Lord Who created. Recite that **your** Lord is the most Generous and that to **your** Lord is the returning.

96:9-10 Have **you yourself** considered he who prohibits a servant when he invokes blessings?

96:11-12 Have **you** considered if he had been on guidance or commanded God-consciousness?

96:13 Have **you** considered if he denied and turned away? Knows he not that God sees? No indeed!

96:19 No indeed! Truly, obey **you** him not but prostrate **yourself** to God and be near to Him.

> God asks him: Have **you** considered those who prohibit a servant from invoking blessings? Have **you** considered if he had been on guidance or commanded God-consciousness, yet there are those who prohibit the servant of God from doing this? Have **you** considered if someone denies the message and turns away? Does such a person not know that God sees him? The reply to the question: No, indeed. If such a person does not refrain himself, God will lay hold of him by his hair. Have this person call to his assembly. God will call forth the guards of hell. No, indeed. Do not obey this

person, but continue to prostrate **your**self to God and be near to Him.

2. CHAPTER 68: THE PEN (AL-QALAM)

68:2 **You**, (Muhammad), are not, by the divine blessing of **your** Lord, one who is possessed.

68:3 Truly, there is for **you** (Muhammad) certainly, compensation, that which is unfailing.

68:4 Truly, **you**, (Muhammad), are of sublime morals.

68:5-6 **You**, (Muhammad), will perceive and they will perceive which of you is demented.

68:7 Truly, **your** Lord, (Muhammad), He is greater in knowledge of whoever went astray from His Way and He is greater in knowledge of ones who are truly guided.

> **You** (Muhammad) are not one who is possessed, but one who has received a divine blessing. **You** are one who will receive an unfailing compensation. **You** are of sublime morals. **You** will see and those who are ungrateful will see. **Your** Lord is greater in knowledge of whoever went astray from His Way and He is greater in knowledge of ones who are truly guided.

68:9 They (the ungrateful) wished that **you**, (Muhammad), would compromise with them and they would compromise with **you**.

68:10-13 Obey **you** not, (Muhammad), the worthless swearer, defamer, one who goes about with slander, slandering, one who delays good, is a sinful aggressor, cruel and, after that, dishonorable (unworthy, base, shameful) because he has been possessor of wealth and children.

> The ungrateful had wished that **you** would compromise with this and then they would have compromised with **you**. Muhammad is cautioned: Do not obey contemptible people who always swear an oath to the truth of their statement because they feel they will not be taken at their word nor do their actions accord with their words.

68:46 Or have you, (Muhammad), asked them for a compensation, so that they would be weighed down from something owed?

68:51 It was almost as if those who were ungrateful looked at **you**, (Muhammad), sternly with their sight when they heard the Remembrance, and they say: He is one who is possessed!

> It is almost as if those who were ungrateful looked at **you** sternly when they heard a Remembrance (*dhikr*), a Reminder, and they say: He, Muhammad, is one who is possessed. Little do they know that it is a Reminder for all the worlds and all the beings.

3. CHAPTER 73: THE ONE WHO IS WRAPPED (AL-MUZZAMMIL)

73:1 O **you**, (Muhammad), the one who is wrapped.

73:5 We will cast on **you**, (Muhammad), a weighty saying.

73:7 Truly, for **you**, (Muhammad), in the daytime is a lengthy occupation.

73:8 Remember **you**, (Muhammad), the Name of **your** Lord. Devote **your**self to Him with total devotion.

73:9 The Lord of the East and of the West, there is no god but He. So take Him to **your**self as **your** Trustee.

73:20 Truly, **your** Lord knows that **you**, (Muhammad), be standing up for nearly two thirds of the nighttime, or a half of it or a third of it, along with a section of those who are with **you**. God ordains the nighttime and the daytime.

O, (Muhammad) who is wrapped! We will cast a weighty saying on **you**. **You** are kept busy for long periods of the day. Remember the Name of **your** Lord and devote **your**self to Him with total devotion. There is no god but He, the Lord of the East and the West, so take Him to **your**self, Muhammad, as **your** trustee. Have patience with regard to what the ungrateful say and abandon them with a graceful abandoning.

4. CHAPTER 74: THE ONE WHO IS WRAPPED IN A CLOAK (AL-MUDDATHTHIR)

74:1 O **you**, (Muhammad), the one who wrapped himself in a cloak!

74:3 Magnify **your** Lord

74:4 Purify **your** garments.

74:7 For **your** Lord, then, have **you**, (Muhammad), patience.

74:27 How will **you**, (Muhammad), recognize what Saqar is?

Your Lord knows that **you** have been standing up for nearly two-thirds of the night or half of it or a third of it along with a group of people who are with **you**. O **you** who wrapped **your**self in a cloak, magnify **your** Lord and purify **your** garments. Have patience. The question then comes: How will **you** recognize what Saqar is? The answer: Saqar does not forsake nor allow anything to remain from its scorching. Over it are nineteen. God has assigned angels to be wardens of the Fire. There number are a test for the ungrateful. However, those who were given the book are reassured and those who believe, add to their belief. Ask those in whose hearts there is a sickness and those who are ungrateful: What does God want by this example? Thus, God causes to go astray whom He wills and He guides whom He wills. None knows the armies of **your** Lord but He. It is only a Reminder for the mortals.

8. CHAPTER 87: THE LOFTY (AL-AALI)

87:1 Glorify the Name of **your** Lord, The Lofty.

87:6 We will make **you**, (Muhammad), recite and **you** will not forget.

87:8 We will make easy for **you** an easing.

Glorify the Name of **your** Lord, the Lofty, Muhammad. We will make **you** recite and **you** will not forget. We will make the way easy for **you**.

10. CHAPTER 89: THE DAWN (AL-FAJR)

89:6 Have **you**, (Muhammad), not considered what **your** Lord accomplished with (the people of Aad).

89:13 **Your** Lord unloosed on them a scourge of punishment.

89:14 Truly, **your** Lord is, surely, on the watch.

89:22 **Your** Lord will draw near, and the angels, ranged in rows.

89:28 Return to **your** Lord, one that is well-pleasing, well-pleased.

89:29 Enter **you**, (Muhammad), among My servants.

89:30 **You**, (Muhammad), enter My Garden!

> Have **you** not considered, Muhammad, what **your** Lord did with the People of Aad? **Your** Lord unleased upon them and the People of Iram and the People of Thamud and the Pharaoh and his people, a great affliction. Truly, **your** Lord is ever watchful. It is **your** Lord who will draw near with the angels ranged in rows. Return to **your** Lord, one who is well-pleasing, well-pleased. The Prophet is told: Enter **you** among My servants and enter **you** My Garden!

11. CHAPTER 93: THE FORENOON (AL-DUHA)

93:3 **Your** Lord deserted **you**, (Muhammad), not, nor is He in hatred of **you**.

93:4 Truly, the last will be better for **you**, (Muhammad), than the first.

93:5 **Your** Lord will give to **you**, (Muhammad). Then, **you** will be well-pleased.

93:6 Found He **you**, (Muhammad), not an orphan and He gave **you** refuge?

93:7 Found He **you**, (Muhammad), one who is looking for guidance, then, He guided **you**?

93:8 Found He **you**, (Muhammad), one who wants, then, He enriched **you**?

93:11 And as for the divine blessing of **your** Lord, divulge it!

> **Your** Lord, Muhammad, has not deserted **you,** nor does He hate **you**. Truly, the last will be better for **you** than the first. **Your** Lord will give to **you**. Then, **you** will be well-pleased. Did He not find **you** an orphan and He gave **you** refuge? Did He not find **you** looking for guidance, then, He guided **you**? Did He not finding you wanting and He enriched **you**? As for the divine blessing of **your** Lord, divulge it!

12. CHAPTER 94: THE EXPANSION (AL-INSHIRAH)

94:1 Expand We not **your** breast,

94:2 and lifted from **you**, (Muhammad), the heavy loaded burden,

94:3 that weighed heavily on **your** back?

94:4 Exalted We not **your** remembrance?

94:7 When **you**, (Muhammad), finished **your** duties, then, work on supplication,

94:8 and quest **your** Lord.

Did We not expand **your** breast? Did We not lift the heavy loaded burden that weighed heavily on **your** back from **you**? Do We not exalt **your** remembrance? When **you** have finished your duties, work on supplication and quest **your** Lord.

15. CHAPTER 108: THE ABUNDANCE (AL-KAWTHAR)

108:1 Truly, We gave **you**, (Muhammad), the abundance.
108:2 Invoke blessings for **your** Lord and make sacrifice.
108:3 Truly, the one who detests **you**, he is the one who is cut off.

17. CHAPTER 107: SMALL KINDNESSES (AL-MAUN)

107:1-107:7 Had **you**, (Muhammad), considered one who denies this way of life?

Had **you** considered one who denies this way of life? That is the one who drives away the orphan with force, who does not urge giving food to the needy. Shame on the ones who offer formal prayer, but are heedless of it, who only do so to show-off and are the ones who forbid small assistance and kindnesses.

19. CHAPTER 105: THE ELEPHANT (AL-FIL)

105:1 Have **you**, (Muhammad), not considered what **your** Lord accomplished with the Companions of the Elephant?

Speaking of the Ethiopian leader, Abraha, attempted attack upon the Kabah in the year 670 CE, the year the Prophet was born, it asks: Have **you** not considered what **your** Lord accomplished with the Companions of the Elephant? Had He not led their cunning to nothing? He sent upon them flocks of birds thowing at them rocks of baked clay. Then He made them like ones who are consumed by husked grain.

23. CHAPTER 53: THE STAR (AL-NAJM)

53:29 So turn **you**, (Muhammad), aside from him who turns away from Our Remembrance and he wants nothing but this present life.
53:30 That is their attainment of the knowledge. Truly, **your** Lord, He is the One Who is greater in knowledge of whoever went astray from His way. He is greater in knowledge of whoever were truly guided.
53:33 Had **you**, (Muhammad), considered him who turned away?
53:42 Towards **your** Lord is the Utmost Boundary.
53:55 Then, which of the benefits of **your** Lord will **you**, (Muhammad), quarrel with?

So, Muhammad, turn **you** aside from him who turns away from Our Remembrance and he wants nothing but this present life. That is the extent of their knowledge. Truly, **your** Lord, He is the One Who is greater in knowledge of those who go astray from His way and He is greater in knowledge of those who are truly guided. Truly, **your** Lord is One Who is Extensive in forgiveness.

24. CHAPTER 80: HE FROWNED (ABASA)

80:3 What will cause **you**, (Muhammad), to recognize so that perhaps he will purify himself?

80:6-80:7 Then, **you** have attended to him. There is not upon **you**, (Muhammad), any blame if he purifies not himself.

80:8-80:10 Yet as for him who drew near to **you**, coming eagerly for knowledge, and he dreads God, **you** have paid no heed to him?

Have **you**, Muhammad, considered him who turned away and gave a little, giving grudgingly? Is the knowledge of the unseen with him so that he sees it? Or is he told what is in the scrolls of Moses and of Abraham who paid his account in full? The Utmost Boundary, the final end, the final destination is towards **your** Lord.

Note: When the Quran says: *He frowned and turned away that the blind man drew near him*, some say that the sign was in reference to the Prophet who frowned and turned away. Others say that the Quran always addresses the Prophet in the second person singular, thou (**you**), and here the Quran says "he."

It was the Quraysh leader who was in discussion with the Prophet who frowned and turned away that the blind man drew near him. Then the Quran address the Prophet: *And what will cause* you *to recognize so that perhaps he* [the Quraysh leader] *will purify himself or yet recollect and a reminder profit him* [the Quraysh leader]? *But as for he who was self-complacent* [the Quraysh leader], then, **you**, Muhammad, *attend to him and not upon* **you**, Muhammad, *is any blame if he* [the Quraysh leader] *purifies not himself. Yet as for him* [the blind man] *who drew near to* **you**, Muhammad, *coming eagerly for knowledge and he dreads God*, then, **you**, Muhammad, *have paid no heed to him* [the blind man]? *No indeed! Truly, this is a Reminder.*

25. CHAPTER 97: THE NIGHT OF POWER (AL-QADR)

97:2 What will cause **you**, (Muhammad), to recognize what is the Night of Power?

97:3 The Night of Power is better than a thousand months.

What will cause **you**, Muhammad, to recognize what the Night of Power is? The answer: The Night of Power is better than a thousand months. The angels come forth and the Spirit during it with their Lord's permission, with every command. Peace it is until the time of the rising dawn.

27. CHAPTER 85: THE CONSTELLATIONS (AL-BURUJ)

85:12 Truly, the seizing by force by **your** Lord is severe.

85:17-18 Approached **you**, (Muhammad), the discourse of the armies of Pharaoh and Thamud?

85:17-85:21: Truly, Muhammad, the seizing by force by **your** Lord is severe. He causes to begin and He causes to return. He is The Forgiving, The Loving, the Possessor of the Glorious Throne, Achiever of what He wants. Has there approached **you**, Muhammad, the discourse of the armies of Pharaoh and of the People of Thamud? Nay! Those who are ungrateful persist in denial. God is One Who Encloses them from behind. Nay! It is a glorious Recitation inscribed on the Guarded Tablet.

28. CHAPTER 95: THE FIG (AL-TIN)

95:7 What will cause **you**, (Muhammad), to deny the Judgment after that?

95:1-95:8: God swears an oath by the fig and the olive, by Mount Sinai, by this trustworthy land: Truly We have created the human being of the fairest symmetry. Moreover, We returned him to the lowest of the low. But those who have believed and the ones who have acted in accord with morality, for them is compensation, that which is unfailing. What will cause **you** to deny the Judgment after that? Is not God the most just of the ones who judge?

30. CHAPTER 101: THE DISASTER (AL-QARIAH)

101:3 What will cause **you**, (Muhammad), to recognize what the Disaster is?

101:10 What will cause **you**, (Muhammad), to recognize what it is?

What will cause **you**, Muhammad, to recognize what the Disaster is? The answer: On a day humanity will be like dispersed moths and the mountains will become like plucked wool clusters, then for him whose balance is heavy will be one whose life is pleasant, well-pleasing. But he whose balance is made light, his abode of rest will be the pit. What will cause **you**, Muhammad, to recognize what it is? It is a hot fire.

31. CHAPTER 75: THE RESURRECTION (AL-QIYAMAH)

75:12 With **your** Lord on this Day will be **your** recourse.

75:16 Impel not **your** tongue to hasten it.

75:18 But when We recited it, follow **you**, (Muhammad), its Recitation.

75:25 **You**, (Muhammad), will think that a crushing calamity has been inflicted on them.

75:30 That Day he will be driving toward **your** Lord

75:1-75:31: God swears an oath by the Day of Resurrection and by the reproaching (*lawwamah*) soul. He says: The human being assumes that We will never gather his bones. Yea! We are ones who have the power to shape his fingers again. Nay! The human being wants to act immorally when faced with it. He asks: When is this Day of Resurrection? But when their sight will be astonished and the moon will cause the earth to be swallowed and the sun and the moon are gathered, the human being will say on that Day: Where is a place to run away to? No indeed! There is no refuge.

On that Day with **your** Lord, Muhammad, will be **your** recourse. Move not **your** tongue, O Muhammad, in repeating the revelations brought **you** by Gabriel, before he shall have finished the same, that **you** may quickly commit them to memory. Truly, upon Us is its collection and its Recitation. When We recited it, follow its Recitation. From Us after that is its clear explanation. Faces on that Day will be ones that beam, ones that look towards their Lord and faces on that Day will be ones that scowl. They will think that a crushing calamity has befallen them. No indeed! When it reaches the collar bone at death and it is asked: Where is one who is a wizard to save me? The question arises because he did not establish The Truth nor did he invoke blessings. That Day the drive will be towards **your** Lord, Muhammad. The person denied the Recitation and turned away. The Quran repeats four times: Woe to you who denied, turned away and went arrogantly to his people.

32. CHAPTER 104: THE SLANDERER (AL-HUMAZAH)

104:5 What will cause **you**, (Muhammad), to recognize what the Crusher is?

104:5-104:9: What will cause **you**, Muhammad, to recognize what the Crusher is? The answer: It is the fire of God that is kindled eternally, perusing the minds finding its way to the innermost being of thoughts and desire that which will be closing in on them with its outstretched, towering pillars.

33. CHAPTER 77: THE ONES WHO ARE SENT (AL-MURASALAT)

77:14 What would cause **you**, (Muhammad), to recognize what the Day of Decision is?

77:8-77:14: And what would cause **you**, Muhammad, to recognize what the Day of Decision is? The answer: When the stars are obliterated and when the heaven is cleaved and when the mountains are scattered to the winds and when the time is set for the Messengers, for which Day are these appointed? For the Day of Decision. Woe on that Day to the ones who deny!

34. CHAPTER 50: QAF (QAF)

50:39 Have **you**, (Muhammad), patience with whatever they say and glorify with the praise of **your** Lord before the coming up of the sun and before sunset.

50:41 Listen **you**, (Muhammad), on a Day when one who calls out will cry out from a near place.

50:45 **You**, (Muhammad), are not haughty over them, so remind by the Quran whoever fears My threat.

50:39-50:45: So, Muhammad, have **you** patience with whatever they say. Glorify **your** Lord with praise before the coming up of the sun and before sunset. Listen, Muhammad, on a Day when one who calls out will cry out from a near place. **You**, Muhammad are not haughty towards them so remind with the Quran whoever fears My threat.

35. Chapter 90: The Land (al-Balad)

90:2 **You**, (Muhammad), are a lodger in this land.

90:12 What will cause **you**, (Muhammad), to recognize what the steep ascent is?

> 90:2-90:18: **You** are a lodger in this land. What will cause **you** to recognize what the steep ascent is? The answer: It is the liberating of a bondsperson or feeding an orphan kin on a day of famine, or a needy person in misery. Moreover, it is to be among those who have believed and counsel one another to patience and counsel one another to clemency. Those will be the Companions of the Right hand. But they who were ungrateful for Our signs, they will be the Companions of the Left Hand and over them a fire that is closing in.

36. Chapter 86: The Night Visitor (al-Tariq)

86:2 What will cause **you**, (Muhammad), to recognize what the Night Visitor is?

> What will cause **you** to recognize what the Night Visitor is? The answer: It is the piercing star. Truly every soul has one who guards it. So let the human being look on of what he was created. He was created of water, that which gushes forth, going forth from between the loins and the breast bone.

86:17 Respite the ones who are ungrateful! Grant **you**, (Muhammad), them a delay for a while.

37. Chapter 54: The Moon (al-Qamar)

54:6 So turn **you** away, (Muhammad), from them on a Day when One Who Calls will call to a horrible thing.

> 54:6-54:8: Turn **you** away from them on a Day when One Who Calls will call to a horrible thing. Their sight will be humbled and they will go forth from the tombs as if they had been dispersed locusts, ones who run forward with their eyes fixed in horror towards The One Who Calls. The ones who are ungrateful will say: This is a difficult Day!

38. Chapter 38: Saad (Saad)

38:9 Or are they owners of the treasures of mercy of **your** Lord, The Almighty, The Giver?

> 38:8-38:10: The ungrateful are in uncertainty about My Remembrance. Nay! They have not experienced My punishment! Or are they owners of the treasures of mercy of **your** Lord, The Almighty, The Giver? Or is theirs the dominion of the heavens and the earth and what is between them?

38:29 It is a blessed Book that We caused to descend to **you**, (Muhammad), so that they meditate on its signs and those imbued with intuition recollect.

It is a blessed Book that We caused to descend to **you** so that they meditate on its signs and those imbued with intuition recollect.

39. CHAPTER 7: THE ELEVATED PLACES (AL-ARAF)

7:2 It is a Book that was caused to descend to **you**, (Muhammad). So let there be no impediment in **your** breast about it so that **you** will warn with it and as a reminder to the ones who believe.

7:101 These are the towns. Their tidings We relate to **you**, (Muhammad). Certainly, their Messengers drew near them with the clear portents. But they had not been believing in what they denied before. Thus, God set a seal on the hearts of the ones who are ungrateful.

7:172 Mention, (Muhammad), when **your** Lord took from the Children of Adam—from their generative organs—their offspring and called to them to witness of themselves: Am I not your Lord? They said: Yea! We bore witness, so that you say not on the Day of Resurrection: Truly, we had been ones who were heedless of this.

7:176 If We willed, We would have exalted (the one in error) with (the messages), but he inclined towards the earth, and followed his own desires. His parable is like the parable of a dog. If **you** will attack it, it pants. Or if **you** will leave it, it pants. That is the parable of the folk, those who denied Our signs. Then, relate these narratives so that perhaps they will reflect.

7:173-7:175: Or they not say: Our fathers before us ascribed partners with God. We had been offspring after them. Shall **You** cause us to perish for what the ones who dealt in falsehood accomplished? Thus, We explain our signs distinctly so that perhaps they would return. Recount to them the tiding of him to whom We gave our signs, but he cast himself off from them. So Satan pursued him. Then he because among the ones who were in error.

7:187 They ask **you**, (Muhammad), about the Hour, when will it berth? Say: The knowledge of that is only with my Lord. None will display its time but He. It was heavy, hidden in the heavens and the earth. It will approach you not but suddenly. They will ask **you**, (Muhammad), as if **you** had been one who is well-informed about it. Say: The knowledge of that is only with God, but most of humanity knows not.

7:198 If you call them to the guidance, they hear not. **You**, (Muhammad), have seen them look on **you**, but they perceive not.

7:199 Take **you**, (Muhammad), what you can spare and command what is honorable. Turn aside from the ones who are ignorant.

7:200 But if enmity is sown by Satan in **you**, (Muhammad), sowing enmity, then, seek refuge in God. Truly, He is Hearing, Knowing.

7:203 When **you**, (Muhammad), have not approached them with a sign, they said: Why had **you** not improvised one? Say: I follow only what is revealed to me from my Lord. This is clear evidence from your Lord and guidance and mercy for a folk who believe.

7:205 Remember **your** Lord in **your**self humbly and with awe instead of openly publishing the sayings at the first part of the day and the eventide. Be **you** not, (Muhammad), among the ones who are heedless.

7:206 Truly, those who are with **your** Lord grow not arrogant from His worship. They glorify Him and they prostrate themselves to Him.

41. CHAPTER 36: YASIN (YA SIN)

36:3 Truly, **you**, (Muhammad), are among the ones who are sent.

36:6 **You**, (Muhammad), warn a folk whose fathers were not warned, so they were ones who were heedless.

36:10 Equal it is to them whether **you**, (Muhammad), warn them, or **you** warn them not. They will not believe.

36:11 **You**, (Muhammad), have only warned whoever followed the Remembrance and dreaded The Merciful in the unseen, so give him good tidings of forgiveness and a generous compensation.

36:13 Propound, (Muhammad), a parable for them: The Companions of the Town when ones who were sent drew near them.

36:76 So let not their saying (that of the ungrateful) dishearten **you**, (Muhammad). Truly, We know what they (the ungrateful) keep secret and what they speak openly.

42. CHAPTER 25: THE CRITERION (AL-FURQAN)

25:9 Look on how they (the ungrateful) propounded for **you**, (Muhammad), parables for they went astray and are not able to find a way.

25:10 Blessed be He Who, had He willed, assigned for **you** better than that, (Muhammad), Gardens beneath which rivers run and He will assign for **you** palaces.

25:16 For them in it will be whatever they will, ones who will dwell in it forever. That had been from **your** Lord a promise, one that will be fulfilled.

25:20 We sent not before **you**, (Muhammad), any ones who are sent but that, truly, they eat food and walk in the markets. We made some of you as a test for some others. Will you endure patiently? **Your** Lord is Seeing.

25:31 We assigned for every Prophet an enemy of the ones who sin. **Your** Lord sufficed as one who guides and as a helper.

25:32 Those who were ungrateful said: Why was the Quran not sent down to him all at once? Thus, We will make firm **your** mind by it. We chanted a chanting.

25:33 They bring **you** no parable. We brought about The Truth to **you**, (Muhammad), and a fairer exposition.

25:41 When they saw **you**, (Muhammad), they mocked **you** (saying): Is this the one whom God raised up as a Messenger?

25:43 Had **you**, (Muhammad), considered him who took to himself his own desires as his god? Would **you**, then, be a trustee over him?

25:44 Or assume **you**, (Muhammad), that most of them (the ungrateful) hear or are reasonable? They are not but as flocks. Nay! They (the ungrateful) are ones who go astray from a way.

25:45 Have **you**, (Muhammad), not considered how **your** Lord stretched out the shade? If He willed, He would make it a place of rest. Again, We made the sun an indicator over it.

25:54 It is He Who created a mortal from water and made for him kindred by blood and kin by marriage. **Your** Lord had been ever Powerful.

25:56 We sent **you**, (Muhammad), as one who gives good tidings and as a warner.

25:58 Put **your** trust in the Living Who is Undying and glorify His praise. He sufficed to be aware of the impieties of His servants.

43. CHAPTER 35: THE ORIGINATOR (AL-FATIR)

35:4 If they deny **you**, (Muhammad), surely, Messengers before **you** were denied. To God all affairs are returned.

35:8 Then, who is there whose direness of his actions was made to appear pleasing to him so that, then, he saw it as fairer? Truly, God causes to go astray whomever He wills and guides whomever He wills. So let not **your** soul be wasted in regret for them. Truly, God is Knowing of what they craft!

35:12 The two bodies of water are not on the same level. This is agreeable, water of the sweetest kind, that which is delicious to drink, and the other is salty, bitter. But from each you eat succulent flesh and pull out glitter that you wear. **You**, (Muhammad), will see the boats, that plow through the waves on it, that you be looking for His grace and so that perhaps you will give thanks.

35:14 If you call to them, they would not hear your supplication. Even if they heard, they would not respond to you. On the Day of Resurrection they will disbelieve in your association with them. None tells **you**, (Muhammad), like One Who is Aware.

35:18 No burdened soul will bear another's load. If one who is weighed down calls for help for his heavy load, nothing of it is carried for him, even if he had been possessor of kinship. Have **you**, (Muhammad), warned only those who dread their Lord in the unseen and performed the formal prayer? He who purified himself, then, only purifies for himself. To God is the Homecoming.

35:22 Nor are the living and the lifeless on the same level. Truly, God causes to hear whom He wills. **You**, (Muhammad), are not one who causes to hear whoever is in graves.

35:23 **You**, (Muhammad), are but a warner.

35:24 Truly, We sent **you**, (Muhammad), with The Truth, a bearer of good tidings and a warner. There is not any community, but a warner passed away among them.

35:25 If they deny **you**, (Muhammad), so, surely, those who were before them denied. Their Messengers drew near them with the clear portents and with the Psalms and the illuminating Book.

35:27 Have **you**, (Muhammad), not considered that God caused water to descend from the heavens? Then, We brought out fruits, the ones of varying hues. Among the mountains are white and red streaks—the ones of varying hues—and others raven black.

35:31 What We revealed to **you**, (Muhammad), of the Book is The Truth, that establishes as true what was in advance of it. Truly, God is Aware, Seeing of His servants.

35:42-35:43: They swore by God the most earnest oaths, that if a warner drew near to them, they would be better guided than any of the other communities. Yet. when a warner drew near to them, it increased nothing in them but aversion, growing arrogant on the earth and planning evil deeds. The plan of bad deeds surround none but people themselves. Then, do they expect any a way but that of the ancient ones? **You**, (Muhammad), will never find in a way of God any substitution. **You** will never find in the way of God any revision.

44. CHAPTER 19: MARY (MARYAM)

19:38 How well **you** hear! How well they will hear! How well **you** perceive on that Day they will approach Us, but today the ones who are unjust are in a clear wandering astray!

19:39 Warn **you** them, (Muhammad), of the Day of Regret when the command would be decided. Yet, they are heedless and they believe not.

19:65 ... the Lord of the heavens and the earth, and what is between them! So worship Him and maintain **you**, (Muhammad), patience in His worship. Have **you** known any namesake for Him?

19:76 God increases in guidance those who were truly guided and endure in accord with morality. They are better with **your** Lord in reward for good deeds and better for turning back.

19:77 Had **you**, (Muhammad), seen him who was ungrateful for Our signs, who said: Will I be given wealth and children?

19:83-84 Have **you**, (Muhammad), not considered that We sent the satans against the ones who were ungrateful to confound them with confusion? So hasten **you**, (Muhammad), not against them. We only number for them a sum (of days).

19:97 So, truly, We made this easy on **your** tongue. Certainly, **you**, (Muhammad), will give good tidings with it to the ones who are Godfearing and **you** will warn a most stubborn folk with it.

19:98 How many a generation caused We to perish before them? Are you, (Muhammad), conscious of anyone of them or hear you so much as a whisper from them?

45. Chapter 20: Ta Ha (Ta Ha)

20:2 We caused not the Quran to descend to you, (Muhammad), that you be in despair.

20:7 If you, (Muhammad), are to publish a saying, yet, truly, He knows the secret and what is more secret.

20:99 Thus, We relate to you, (Muhammad), some tiding of what preceded. Surely, We gave you, (Muhammad), from Our Presence, a Remembrance.

20:105 They will ask you, (Muhammad), about the mountains. Then, say: My Lord will scatter them a scattering.

20:107 Then, you, (Muhammad), will see not in it any crookedness nor unevenness.

20:108 On that Day they will follow one who calls. There will be no crookedness in him. Voices will be hushed for The Merciful, so you, (Muhammad), will hear nothing but a murmuring.

20:114 Then, exalted be God, The True King, and hasten not the Recitation before its revelation is decreed to you. Say: My Lord! Increase me in knowledge!

20:129 If a Word preceded not from your Lord for a term that was determined, it would be close at hand.

20:130 So have you, (Muhammad), patience with what they say and glorify the praises of your Lord before the coming up of the sun and before sunset and during the nighttime night watch and glorify at the end of the daytime, so that perhaps you will be well-pleased.

20:131 Stretch not out your eyes for what We gave of enjoyment in this life to spouses among them as the luster of this present life so that We try them by it. Provision of your Lord is Best and that which endures.

20:132 Command your people to the formal prayer, and to maintain patience in it. We ask not of you, (Muhammad), for any provision. We provide for you and the Ultimate End will be for the God-conscious.

46. Chapter 56: The Inevitable (al-Waqiah)

56:74 Then, glorify with the name of your Lord, The Sublime.

56:91 Peace for you, (Muhammad), from the Companions of the Right.

56:96 So glorify the Name of your Lord, The Almighty.

47. Chapter 26: The Poets (al-Shuara)

26:3 Perhaps you, (Muhammad), would be one who consumes yourself in grief because they (the ungrateful) become not ones who believe.

26:9 Truly, **your** Lord, He is, certainly, The Almighty, The Compassionate.

26:192-26:195: This, truly, is the sending down successively of the Lord of the worlds that the Trustworthy Spirit has brought down on **your** heart that **you**, (Muhammad), be among the one who warn in a clear Arabic tongue.

26:205-26:207 Had **you**, (Muhammad), considered that if We gave them enjoyment for years and there drew near to them what they have been promised, they would not be able to make use of what they had been given of enjoyment?

26:213 So call **you**, (Muhammad), not to any god with God so that **you** be among the ones who are punished.

26:214 Warn **your** nearest kin, the kinspeople.

26:215 Make low **your** wing to whoever followed **you**, (Muhammad), among the ones who believe.

26:216 Then, if they rebelled against **you**, (Muhammad), then, say: Truly, I am free of what you do.

26:217 Put **your** trust in The Almighty, The Compassionate,

26:218-26:219 Who sees **you**, (Muhammad), at the time **you** stand up, and **your** going to and fro among the ones who prostrate themselves.

26:225-26:226: Have **you**, (Muhammad), not considered that they wander in every valley and that they say what they do not accomplish?

48. CHAPTER 27: THE ANT (AL-NAML)

27:6 Truly, **you**, **you**, (Muhammad), are in receipt of the Quran from the Presence of the Wise, Knowing.

27:70 Feel **you**, (Muhammad), not remorse for them, nor be troubled by what they plan.

27:73 Truly, **your** Lord is Possessor of Grace for humanity, but most of them give not thanks.

27:74 Truly, **your** Lord knows what their breasts hide and what they speak openly.

27:78 Truly, **your** Lord will decree between them with His determination. He is The Almighty, The Knowing.

27:79 So put **your** trust in God. Truly, **you**, (Muhammad), are on The Clear Truth.

27:80 Truly, **you**, (Muhammad), will not cause the dead to hear nor will **you** cause to hear the unwilling to hear the calling to them when they turned as ones who draw back.

27:81 Nor will **you**, (Muhammad), be one who guides the unwilling to see out of their fallacy. **You** will not cause to hear, but whoever believes in Our signs and so they are ones who submit to God.

27:88 **You**, (Muhammad), will see the mountains **you** have assumed to be that which are fixed. But they will pass by as the passing of the clouds.

This is the handiwork of God Who created everything very well. Truly, He is Aware of what you accomplish.

27:93 Say: The Praise belongs to God. He will cause you to see His signs and you will recognize them. **Your** Lord is not One Who is Heedless of what you do.

49. Chapter 28: The Story (al-Qasas)

28:50 If they (the ungrateful) respond not to **you**, (Muhammad), then, know that they only follow their own desires. Who is one who goes further astray than one who followed his own desires without guidance from God? Truly, God guides not the folk, the ones who are unjust.

28:56 Truly, **you**, (Muhammad), have not guided whom **you** have loved, but God guides whomever He wills. He is greater in knowledge of the ones who are truly guided.

28:57 They (the ungrateful) said: If we follow the guidance with **you**, (Muhammad),we would be snatched away from our region. (The response): Establish We not firmly for them a holy, safe place where all kinds of fruits are collected as provision from Our Presence? But most of them know not.

28:59 **Your** Lord had not been One Who Causes towns to perish until He raises up to their mother-town a Messenger who recounts Our signs to them. We never had been Ones Who Cause towns to perish unless their people are ones who are unjust.

28:68 **Your** Lord creates whatever He wills and chooses. Not for them had there been a choice. Glory be to God and exalted is He above partners they ascribe!

28:69 **Your** Lord knows what their breasts hide and what they speak openly.

28:85 Truly, He Who imposed the Quran for **you**, (Muhammad), will be one who restores **you** to the place of return. Say: My Lord is greater in knowledge of whoever drew near guidance and whoever is clearly wandering astray.

28:86 **You**, (Muhammad), had been without hope that the Book would be cast down to **you**, but as a mercy from **your** Lord. Be **you** not a sustainer of the ones who are ungrateful.

28:87 Let them not bar **you**, (Muhammad), from the signs of God after they were caused to descend to **you**. Call to **your** Lord. Be **you** not among the ones who are polytheists.

50. Chapter 17: The Journey by Night (al-Isra)

17:14 Recite **your** book! This day **your** soul sufficed **you**, (Muhammad), as **your** reckoner against **you**.

17:17 How many generations have We caused to perish after Noah? **Your** Lord sufficed as Aware, Seeing the impieties of His servants.

17:20 To each We furnish relief, these and these, with the gift of **your** Lord. This gift of **your** Lord is not restricted.

17:23 Your Lord decreed that you worship none but Him! Kindness to the ones who are one's parents. If they reach old age with **you**—one of them or both of them—then, **you** will not say to them a word of disrespect nor scold them, but say a generous saying to them.

17:24 Make **your**self low to them, the wing of the sense of humility through mercy. Say: O my Lord! Have mercy on them even as they raised me when I was small.

17:28 If **you** have turned aside from them, looking for mercy from **your** Lord for which **you** have hoped, then, say to them a saying softly.

17:30 Truly, **your** Lord extends the provision for whom He wills and He tightens for whom He wills. Truly, He, He had been Aware, Seeing of His servants.

17:45 When **you**, (Muhammad), recited the Quran, We made between **you** and between those who believe not in the world to come a partition obstructing their vision.

17:46 We laid sheaths on their hearts so that they not understand it and heaviness in their ears. When **you**, (Muhammad), had remembered **your** Lord in the Quran that He is One, they turned their backs in aversion.

17:47 We are greater in knowledge of what they listen for when they listen to **you**, (Muhammad). When they conspire secretly, the ones who are unjust say: You follow but a bewitched man.

17:48 Look on how they (the ungrateful) propounded parables for **you**, (Muhammad). So they went astray and they are not able to be on a way.

17:50-17:51: Say: Should you be rocks or iron or any creation that is more troublesome in your breasts to raise up? Then, they will say: Who will cause us to return? Say: He Who originated you the first time. Then, they will nod their heads at **you**, (Muhammad), and ask: When will it be? Say: Perhaps it is near.

17:54 **Your** Lord is greater in knowledge of you. If He wills, He will have mercy on you. If He wills, He will punish you. We sent **you** not as a trustee over them.

17:55 **Your** Lord is greater in knowledge of whoever is in the heavens and in and on the earth. Certainly, We gave advantage to some of the Prophets over others. To David We gave Psalms.

17:57 Those to whom they call (the angels) are themselves looking for an approach to their Lord—even those who are near—and they hope for His mercy and they fear His punishment. Truly, the punishment of **your** Lord had been one to fear.

17:60 Mention when We said to **you**, (Muhammad): Truly, **your** Lord enclosed humanity. We made not the dream that We caused **you**, (Muhammad), to see, but as a test for humanity—and the tree (Zaqqum)—one that was cursed in the Quran. We frighten them, but it only increases them in great defiance.

17:84 Say: Each does according to his same manner. **Your** Lord is greater in knowledge of him who is better guided on the way.

17:85 They will ask **you**, (Muhammad), about the spirit. Say: The spirit is of the command of **my** Lord. You were not given the knowledge but a little.

17:86 If We willed, We would, certainly, take away what We revealed (through the spirit) to **you**, (Muhammad). Then, **you** would not find concerning it any trustee (intercessor, pleader) for **you** against Us.

Muhammad, **you** are not, as the ungrateful allege, the author of The Recitation (The Quran). It is only We Who reveal it through the spirit. If We willed, We could certainly take away what We have revealed to you by removing it from the hearts and memory of **you** and those who have memorized it, and from any written record of it. Then you would find for **yourself** no protecting guardian against Us to help **you** to claim or recover it.

17:87 (**You** are spared) by a mercy from **your** Lord. Truly, His grace had been great upon **you**, (Muhammad).

17:90 They (the ungrateful) would say: We will never believe in **you**, (Muhammad), until **you** have a fountain gush out of the earth for us.

17:91 Or will there be a garden for **you**, (Muhammad), of date palms and grapevines that **you** cause rivers to gush forth in its midst with a gushing forth?

17:92 Or have **you**, (Muhammad), caused heaven to drop on us in pieces as **you** had claimed? Or have **you** brought God and the angels as a warranty?

17:93 Or is there a house of ornament for **you**? Or have **you** ascended up into heaven? We will not believe in **your** ascension until **you** have sent down for us a Book that we recite. Say, (Muhammad): Glory be to my Lord! Had I been but a mortal Messenger?

17:97 He whom God guides is one who is truly guided. Whomever He causes to go astray, **you**, (Muhammad), will never find for them protectors other than Him. We will assemble them on the Day of Resurrection on their faces, unseeing and unspeaking and unhearing. Their place of shelter will be hell. Whenever it declined, We will increase the blaze for them.

17:105 We caused it to descend with The Truth. It came down with the Truth. We sent it to **you**, (Muhammad), as one who gives good tidings and as a warner.

17:106 It is a Recitation. We separated it in order that **you**, (Muhammad), recite it to humanity at intervals. We sent it down, a sending successively down.

17:110 Say: Call to God or call to the Merciful. By whatever you call Him, to Him are the Fairer Names. Be **you**, (Muhammad), not loud in **your** formal prayer nor speak in a low tone and look for a way between.

51. CHAPTER 10: JONAH (YUNUS)

10:2 These are the signs of the wise Book. Had it been for humanity to wonder that We revealed to a man from among them that: Warn humanity and give **you**, (Muhammad), good tidings to those who believed so that they will have a sound footing with their Lord? The ones who are ungrateful said: Truly, this is one who is a clear sorcerer.

10:19 Humanity had not been but one community, but, then, they became at variance. If it were not for a Word that preceded from **your** Lord, it would be decided between them immediately about what they are at variance in it.

10:33 Thus, was the Word of **your** Lord realized against those who disobeyed that they will not believe.

10:41 If they denied **you**, (Muhammad), then, **you** say: For me are my actions and for you are your actions. You are free of what I do and I am free of what you do.

10:42 Among them are some who listen to **you**, (Muhammad). So have **you** caused someone unwilling to hear, to hear if they had not been reasonable?

10:43 Among them are some who look on **you**, (Muhammad). So have **you** guided the unwilling to see if they had not been perceiving?

10:46 Whether We cause **you**, (Muhammad), to see some of what We promise them or We call **you** to Us, then, to Us is their return. Again, God will be witness to what they accomplish.

10:53 They ask **you**, (Muhammad), to be told: Is it true? Say, (Muhammad): Yes! By my Lord it is The Truth and you are not ones who frustrate Him.

10:61 Neither have **you**, (Muhammad), been on any matter nor have **you** recounted from the Recitation nor are you doing any action, but We had been ones who bear witness over you when you press on it. Nothing escapes from **your** Lord of the weight of an atom in or on the earth nor in the heaven nor what is smaller than that nor what is greater than that, but it is in a clear Book.

10:65 Let not their saying dishearten **you**, (Muhammad). Truly, all great glory belongs to God. He is The Hearing, The Knowing.

10:99 If **your** Lord willed, all who are on the earth altogether would have believed. Would **you**, (Muhammad), compel humanity against their will until they become ones who believe?

10:105 Set **your** face to the way of life of a monotheist. Be **you** not, (Muhammad), among the ones who are polytheists.

10:106 Call not to other than God what neither profits nor hurts **you**, (Muhammad). If **you** were to accomplish that, truly, **you** would be among the ones who are unjust.

10:107 If God afflicts **you**, (Muhammad), with harm, there is no one who removes it but He. If He wants good for **you**, there is no one who repels His grace. It lights on whomever He wills of His servants. He is The Forgiving, The Compassionate.

10:109 Follow **you**, (Muhammad), what is revealed to **you**. Have **you** patience until God gives judgment. He is Best of the ones who judge.

52. CHAPTER 11: HUD (HUD)

11:7 It is He Who created the heavens and the earth in six days. His Throne had been upon the waters that He try you—which of you is fairer in actions. If **you**, (Muhammad), were to say to them: Truly, you are ones who will be raised up after death, those who were ungrateful would be sure to say: This is nothing but clear sorcery.

11:12 So would **you**, (Muhammad), perhaps be one who leaves some of what is revealed to **you**? Or is **your** breast that which is narrowed by it because they say: Why was a treasure not caused to descend to him or an angel drew near him? Truly, **you** are only a warner. God is a Trustee over everything. Or they say: He devised it.

11:17 Is he, then, who had been on a clear portent from his Lord, and recounts it from Him as one who bears witness—and before it was the Book of Moses, a leader and a mercy—like them? Those believe in it. Whoever is ungrateful for it among the confederates, he is promised the fire! So be **you**, (Muhammad), not hesitant about it. Truly, it is The Truth from **your** Lord, except most of humanity believes not.

11:100 That is from the tidings of the towns that We relate to **you**. Of them, some are ones that are standing up and some are stubble.

11:101 It was not that We did wrong to them. Rather, they did wrong themselves. Their gods whom they call to besides God availed them not at all. When the command of **your** Lord drew near, they increased them not other than in ruination.

11:102 Thus, is the taking of **your** Lord when He took the towns while they are ones who are unjust. Truly, His taking is painful, severe.

11:107 Ones who will dwell in it for as long as the heavens and the earth continued, but what **your** Lord willed. Truly, **your** Lord is Achiever of what He wants.

11:108 As for those who were happy, they will be in the Garden, ones who will dwell in it for as long as the heavens and the earth continued, but what **your** Lord willed, a gift that will not be that which is broken.

11:109 So be **you**, (Muhammad), not hesitant as to what these worship. They worship nothing but what their fathers worshiped before. We are the ones who pay their share in full without being that which is reduced.

11:110 Certainly, We gave Moses the Book, but they were at variance about it. If it were not for a Word that preceded from **your** Lord, it would be decided between them. Truly, they were uncertain about it, ones in grave doubt.

11:111 Truly, to each his account will be paid in full by **your** Lord for their actions. Truly, He is Aware of what they do.

11:112 So go **you**, (Muhammad), straight as **you** were commanded and those who repented with **you** and be not defiant. Truly, He is Seeing of what you do.

11:115 Have **you**, (Muhammad), patience, for, truly, God wastes not the compensation of the ones who are doers of good.

11:117 **Your** Lord had not been causing the towns to perish unjustly while their people are ones who make things right.

11:118-11:119 If **your** Lord willed, He would have made humanity one community. But they cease not to be ones who are at variance, but on whom **your** Lord had mercy. For that, He created them, and the Word of **your** Lord was completed. Certainly, I will fill hell with genie and humanity one and all.

11:120 All that We relate to **you**, (Muhammad), of the tidings of the Messengers is so that We make **your** mind firm by it. The Truth drew near **you** in this, and an admonishment and a reminder for the ones who believe.

11:123 To God belongs the unseen of the heavens and the earth. To Him is the return of every command, so worship Him and put **your** trust in Him. **Your** Lord is not One Who is Heedless of what you do.

54. CHAPTER 15: THE ROCKY TRACT (AL-HIJR)

15:6-15:10 They (the ungrateful) say: O **you**, (Muhammad), to whom was sent down the Remembrance, truly, **you** are one who is possessed. Why have **you**, (Muhammad), not brought angels to us if **you** had been the ones who are sincere? We send angels down not but with The Truth. They (the ungrateful) will not be ones who are given respite. Truly, We, We have sent down the Remembrance and, truly, We are ones who guard it. Certainly, We sent Messengers before **you**, (Muhammad), to partisans of the ancient ones.

15:25 Truly, **your** Lord is He Who assembles. Truly, He is Wise, Knowing.

15:28 And mention when **your** Lord said to the angels: Truly, I am One Who is Creator of mortals out of earth-mud of soft wet earth.

15:86 Truly, **your** Lord is The Knowing Creator.

15:87 Certainly, We gave **you**, (Muhammad), seven often repeated parts of the sublime (*azim*) Quran.

15:88 Stretch not out **your** eyes for what We gave of enjoyment in this life to spouses among them, nor feel remorse for them, but make low **your** wing in kindness to the ones who believe.

15:92 So by **your** Lord, We will, certainly, ask them one and all.

15:94 So call aloud what **you**, (Muhammad), are commanded: Turn aside from the ones who are polytheists!

15:95 Truly, We sufficed **you**, (Muhammad), against the ones who ridicule.

15:97 Certainly, We know that **your** breast became narrowed, injured in spirit, because of what they say.

15:98-15:99 So glorify the praises of **your** Lord and be among the ones who prostrate themselves, and worship **your** Lord until the certainty approaches **you**, (Muhammad).

55. CHAPTER 6: THE FLOCKS (AL-ANAM)

6:7 If We sent down to **you**, (Muhammad), a Book on parchment, then, they (the ungrateful) would have stretched towards it with their hands. Those who were ungrateful would have said: This is nothing but clear sorcery.

6:10 Certainly, Messengers were ridiculed before **you**. So those who derided them were surrounded by what they had been ridiculing.

6:14 Say: Will I take to myself, other than God, a protector, One Who is Originator of the heavens and the earth? It is He who feeds and He who is never fed. Say: Truly, I was commanded that I be the first who submitted to the One God. **You**, (Muhammad), have not been among the ones who are polytheists.

6:17 If God touches **you**, (Muhammad), with harm, then, no one will remove it but He. If He touches **you** with good, then, He is Powerful over everything.

6:25 Among them are those who listen to **you**, (Muhammad). But We laid sheathes on their hearts so that they not understand it and in their ears is a heaviness. If they are to see every sign they will not believe in it. So that when they drew near **you**, they dispute with **you**. Those who were ungrateful say: This is nothing but fables of the ancient ones.

6:27 If **you**, (Muhammad), would see when they would be stationed by the fire, they will say: Would that we be returned to life. Then, we would not deny the signs of our Lord and we would be among the ones who believe.

6:30 If **you**, (Muhammad), would see when they would be stationed before their Lord. He would say: Is this not The Truth? They would say: Yea, by Our Lord. He would say: Then, experience the punishment for what you had been ungrateful.

6:33 Surely, We know that what they say disheartens **you**, (Muhammad). Truly, they deny **you** not. Rather the ones who are unjust negate the signs of God.

6:34 Certainly, Messengers before **you**, (Muhammad), were denied, yet they endured patiently when they were denied. They were maligned until Our help approached them. No one will change the Word of God. Certainly, there drew near **you** tidings of the ones who are sent.

6:35 If their turning aside had been troublesome to **you**, (Muhammad), then, if **you** were able, be looking for a hole in the earth or a ladder to heaven so that **you** would bring them some sign. If God willed, He would have gathered them to The Guidance. Be **you** not among the ones who are ignorant.

6:42 Certainly, We sent to communities that were before **you**, (Muhammad). Then, We took them with desolation and tribulation so that perhaps they will lower themselves to Us.

6:52 Drive not away those who call to their Lord in the morning and the evening, wanting His Countenance. Their reckoning is not on **you**, (Muhammad), at all. **Your** reckoning is not on them at all. If **you** were to drive them away, then, **you** would be among the ones who are unjust.

6:54 When drew near **you**, (Muhammad), those who believe in Our signs, say: Peace be to you. Your Lord prescribed mercy for Himself so that anyone of you who did evil in ignorance—again, repented afterwards and made things right—then, truly, He is Forgiving, Compassionate.

6:66 **Your** folk denied it. It is The Truth. Say: I am not a trustee over you.

6:68 When **you**, (Muhammad), had seen those who engage in idle talk about Our signs, then, turn aside from them until they discuss in conversation other than that. If Satan should cause **you** to forget, then, after a reminder, sit not with the folk, the ones who are unjust.

6:92 This is a Book We caused to descend—that which is blessed—and that which establishes as true what was before it and for **you**, (Muhammad), to warn the Mother of Towns and those who are around it. Those who believe in the world to come, believe in it. They are watchful over their formal prayers.

6:104-6:105 Surely clear evidence has drawn near to you from your Lord. So whoever perceives, it is for his own soul. Whoever is in darkness, it will be against his own soul. Say: I am not a guardian over you. Thus, We diversify the signs and they (the ungrateful) will say: **You**, (Muhammad), have received instruction (from others). (The Quranic response): We will make it (The Recitation) clear for a folk who know.

6:106 Follow **you** what was revealed to **you** from **your** Lord. There is no god but He. Turn **you** aside from the ones who are polytheists.

6:107 If God willed, they would not have ascribed partners with Him. We made **you**, (Muhammad), not a guardian over them, nor are **you** a trustee for them.

6:112 Thus, We made an enemy for every Prophet, satans from among humankind and the jinn. Some of them reveal to some others an ornamented saying, a delusion. If **your** Lord willed, they would not have accomplished it. So forsake them and what they devise,

6:115 Completed was the Word of **your** Lord in sincerity and justice. There is no one who changes His Words. He is The Hearing, The Knowing.

6:116 If **you**, (Muhammad), have obeyed most of who are on the earth, they will cause **you** to go astray from the way of God. They follow nothing but opinion and they only guess.

6:117 Truly, **your** Lord is He Who is greater in knowledge of who goes astray from His way. He is greater in knowledge of the ones who are truly guided.

6:119 Why should you not eat of that over which the Name of God was remembered on it? Surely, He explained distinctly to you what He forbade to you unless you were driven by necessity to it. Truly, many cause others to go astray by their desires without knowledge. Truly, **your** Lord, He is greater in knowledge of the ones who exceed the limits.

6:126 This is the path of **your** Lord, one that is straight. Surely, We explained distinctly the signs for a folk who recollect.

6:131 That is because **your** Lord would never be One Who Causes to Perish towns unjustly while their people are ones who are heedless.

6:132 For everyone there are degrees for what they did. **Your** Lord is not One Who is Heedless of what they do.

6:133 **Your** Lord is The Sufficient, Possessor of Mercy. If He wills, He will cause you to be put away and will make a successor after you of whomever He wills, just as He caused you to grow from offspring of other folk.

6:145 Say: I find not in what was revealed to me to taste that which is forbidden to taste, but that it be carrion or blood, that which is shed or the flesh of swine for that, truly, is a disgrace or was hallowed—contrary to moral law—to other than God on it. Then, whoever was driven by necessity other than being one who is willfully disobedient or one who turns away, truly, **your** Lord is Forgiving, Compassionate.

6:147 If they denied **you**, (Muhammad), say: Your Lord is the Possessor of Extensive Mercy. His might is not repelled from the folk, ones who sin.

6:150 Say: Come on! Bring your witnesses who bear witness that God forbade this. Then, if they bore witness, bear you not witness with them. Follow **you**, (Muhammad), not the desires of those who denied Our signs and those who believe not in the world to come. They equate others with their Lord.

6:158 Look they on only that the angels approach them? Or **your** Lord approach them? Or some signs of **your** Lord approach them? On a Day that approach some signs of **your** Lord, belief will not profit a person if he believed not before, nor earned good because of his belief. Say: Wait awhile! We too are ones who are waiting awhile!

6:159 Truly, those who separated and divided their way of life and had been partisans, be **you**, (Muhammad), not concerned with them at all. Truly, their affair is only with God. Again, He will tell them what they had been accomplishing.

6:165 It is He who made you as viceregents on the earth and exalted some of you above some others in degree that He try you with what He gave you. Truly, **your** Lord is Swift in repayment and He, truly, is Forgiving, Compassionate.

56. CHAPTER 37: THE ONES STANDING IN RANK (AL-SAFFAT)

37:12-37:17: Nay! **You**, (Muhammad), marveled while they derided. When they are reminded, they remember not. When they see a sign, they scoff at it. They say: This is nothing but clear sorcery. (They ask): Is it when we are dead and have become earth dust and bones that we will truly be ones who are raised up and also our fathers, the ancient ones?

57. Chapter 31: Luqman (Luqman)

31:23 Whoever was ungrateful, let not his ingratitude dishearten **you**, (Muhammad). To Us is their return and We will tell them what they did. Truly, God is Knowing of what is in the breasts.

31:25 If **you**, (Muhammad), had asked them who created the heavens and the earth, they will certainly say: God! Say: The Praise belongs to God! But most of them know not.

31:31 Have **you**, (Muhammad), not considered that the boats run through the sea by the divine blessing of God that He causes you to see His signs? Truly in that are signs for every enduring, grateful one.

58. Chapter 34: Sheba (al-Saba)

34:28 We sent **you**, (Muhammad), not, but collectively for humanity as a bearer of good tidings and a warner, but most of humanity knows not.

34:31 Those who were ungrateful said: We will never believe in this, the Quran, nor in what was in advance of it. If **you**, (Muhammad), could but see when the ones who are unjust are stationed before their Lord reproaching one another. Those who were taken advantage of due to their weakness say to those who grew arrogant: If it were not for you, we would have been ones who believe.

34:44 We gave them (the ungrateful) not any Books that they study them nor sent We to them any warner before **you**, (Muhammad).

34:51 If **you**, (Muhammad), would see when they would be terrified, when there is no escape and they would be taken from a near place.

59. Chapter 39: The Troops (al-Zumar)

39:2 Truly, We caused to descend to **you**, (Muhammad), the Book with The Truth so worship God as one who is sincere and devoted in the way of life to Him.

39:19 Against whom was realized the word of punishment? Will **you**, (Muhammad), be saving him from the fire?

39:21 Have **you**, (Muhammad), not considered that God caused to descend water from heaven and threaded fountains in the earth, again, brings out crops by it of hues, ones that are at variance? Again, they wither so **you**, (Muhammad), see them as ones that are growing yellow. Again, He makes them chaff. Truly, in this is a reminder for those imbued with intuition.

39:30 Truly, **you**, (Muhammad), are mortal and, truly, they are mortal.

39:36 Is not God One Who Suffices for His servants? They frighten **you**, (Muhammad), with those other than Him. Whom God causes to go astray, there is not for him any one who guides.

39:38 Truly, if **you**, (Muhammad), had asked them: Who created the heavens and the earth? They would, certainly, say: God. Say: Considered you what you call to other than God? If God wanted some harm for **me**, would they (f) (the female angels) be ones who remove His harm from **me**? Or if He wanted mercy for **me** would they (f) (the female angels) be ones who hold back His mercy? Say: God is enough for **me**. In Him put their trust the ones who put their trust.

39:41 Truly, We caused the Book to descend to **you**, (Muhammad), for humanity with The Truth. So whoever was truly guided, it is only for himself. Whoever went astray, goes astray but for himself. **You** are not over them a trustee.

39:60 On the Day of Resurrection **you**, (Muhammad), will see those who lied against God, their faces, ones that are clouded over. Is there not in hell a place of lodging for ones who increase in pride?

39:75 **You**, (Muhammad), will see the angels as ones who encircle around the Throne glorifying their Lord with praise. It would be decided in Truth among them. It would be said: The Praise belongs to God, the Lord of the worlds.

60. Chapter 40: The One Who Forgives (al-Ghafir)

40:4 No one disputes the signs of God, but those who were ungrateful. So be **you**, (Muhammad), not disappointed with their going to and fro in the land.

40:6 Thus, was the Word of **your** Lord realized against those who were ungrateful that they will be the Companions of the Fire.

40:55 So have **you**, (Muhammad), patience. Truly, the promise of God is true. Ask for forgiveness for **your** impiety. Glorify **your** Lord with praise in the evening and the early morning.

40:69 Have **you**, (Muhammad), not considered those who dispute about the signs of God, where they are turned away?

40:77 So have **you**, (Muhammad), patience. Truly, the promise of God is true. And whether We cause **you** to see some part of what We promise them or We call **you** to Us, then, it is to Us they will be returned.

40:78 Certainly, We sent Messengers before **you**, (Muhammad), among whom We related to **you** and of whom We relate not to **you**. It had not been for any Messenger that he bring a sign, except with the permission of God. So when the command of God drew near, the matter would be decided rightfully. Lost here are these, the ones who deal in falsehood.

61. Chapter 41: They Were Explained Distinctly (al-Fussilat)

41:5 They said: Our hearts are sheathed from that to which **you**, (Muhammad), have called us and in our ears is a heaviness and between us and between **you** is a partition. So work. Truly, we, too, are ones who work.

41:34 Not on the same level are benevolence or the evil deed. Drive back with what is fairer. Then, behold he who between **you**, (Muhammad), and between him was enmity as if he had been a protector, a loyal friend.

41:36 But if Satan sows enmity, sowing enmity in **you**, (Muhammad), then, seek refuge in God. Truly, He is The Hearing, The Knowing.

41:38 But if they grew arrogant, then, those who are with **your** Lord glorify Him during the nighttime and the daytime and they never grow weary.

41:39 Among His signs are that **you**, (Muhammad), have seen the earth as that which is humble. But when We caused water to descend to it, it quivered and swelled. Truly, He Who gives life to it is the One Who Gives Life to the dead. Truly, He is Powerful over everything.

41:43 Nothing is said to **you**, (Muhammad), but what, truly, was said to the Messengers before **you**. Truly, **your** Lord is, certainly, the Possessor of Forgiveness, and the Possessor of Painful Repayment.

41:45 Certainly, We gave Moses the Book. Then, they were at variance about it. If it were not for a Word that had preceded from **your** Lord, it would have been decided between them. But, truly, they are in uncertainty, ones in grave doubt about it.

41:46 Whoever did as one in accord with morality, it is for himself. Whoever did evil, it is against himself. **Your** Lord is not unjust to His servants.

41:53 We will cause them to see Our signs on the horizons and within themselves until it becomes clear to them that it is The Truth. Suffices not **your** Lord that, truly, He is Witness over all things?

62. CHAPTER 42: THE CONSULTATION (AL-SHURA)

42:3 Thus, He reveals to **you**, (Muhammad), and to those who were before **you**, God is The Almighty, The Wise.

42:6 As for those who took to themselves other than Him as protectors, God is Guardian over them and **you**, (Muhammad), are not a Trustee over them.

42:7 Thus, We revealed to **you**, (Muhammad), an Arabic Recitation that **you** will warn the Mother of the Towns and whoever is around it. Warn of the Day of Amassing. There is no doubt about it. A group of people will be in the Garden and a group of people will be in the blaze.

42:13 He laid down the law of the way of life for you, that with which He charged Noah and what We revealed to **you**, (Muhammad), and that with which We charged Abraham and Moses and Jesus. Perform the prescribed way of life and be not split up in it. Troublesome for the ones who are polytheists is that to which **you** have called them. God elects for Himself whomever He wills and guides the penitent to Himself.

42:14 They split not up until after the knowledge drew near them through insolence between themselves. If it were not for a Word that preceded from **your** Lord—until a term, that which is determined—it would be decided between them. Truly, those who were given as inheritance the Book after them are in uncertainty, in grave doubt about it.

42:15 Then, for that, call to this. Go **you**, (Muhammad), straight as **you** were commanded. Follow not their desires. Say: I believed in what God caused to descend from a Book. I was commanded to be just among you. God is our Lord and your Lord. For us are our actions and for you, your actions. There is no disputation between us and between you. God will gather us together. To Him is the Homecoming.

42:17 It is God Who caused the Book to descend with The Truth and the Balance. What causes **you**, (Muhammad), to recognize it so that perhaps the Hour is near?

42:22 **You**, (Muhammad), will see the ones who are unjust as ones who are apprehensive of what they earned and it is that which falls on them. Those who believed and did as the ones in accord with morality are in the well-watered meadows of the Gardens. For them will be whatever they will from their Lord. That it is the great grace.

42:44 Whomever God causes to go astray has no protector apart from Him. **You**, (Muhammad), will see the ones who are unjust when they would see the punishment. They will say: Is there any way of turning it back?

42:45 **You**, (Muhammad), will see them being presented to it as ones who are humbled by a sense of humility, looking on with secretive glances. Those who believed will say: Truly, the ones who are losers are those who lost themselves and their people on the Day of Resurrection. Truly, the ones who are unjust will be in an abiding punishment

42:48 But if they turned aside, We put **you**, (Muhammad), not forward as a guardian over them. For **you** is the delivering of the message. Truly, when We caused the human being to experience mercy from Us, he was glad in it. But when evil deeds light on him—because of what his hands sent—then, truly, the human being is ungrateful.

42:52 Thus, We revealed to **you**, (Muhammad), the Spirit of Our command. **You** had not been informed what the Book is nor what is belief, but We made it a light by which We guide whomever We will of Our servants. Truly, **you**, **you** have guided to a straight path.

63. CHAPTER 43: THE ORNAMENTS (AL-ZUKHRUF)

43:9 Certainly, if **you**, (Muhammad), had asked them: Who created the heavens and the earth? They will, certainly, say: The Almighty, The Knowing created them,.

43:23 Thus, We sent not a warner to any town before **you**, (Muhammad), without ones who are given ease saying: We found our fathers in a community. We are, certainly, ones who imitate their footsteps.

43:32 Would they divide the mercy of **your** Lord? It is We Who divided out among them their livelihood in this present life. Exalted are some of them above some others in degree so that some take to themselves others in their bondage. The mercy of **your** Lord is better than what they gather.

43:40 So have **you**, (Muhammad), caused someone unwilling to hear, to hear or will **you** guide the unwilling to see, or someone who had been clearly going astray?

43:41-42:42 Even if We take **you**, (Muhammad), away, We will, truly, be ones who requite them, or We will cause **you**, (Muhammad), to see what We promised them. Then, We are ones who are omnipotent over them.

43:43 So hold **you**, (Muhammad), fast to what was revealed to **you**. Truly, **you** are on a straight path.

43:44 Truly, this is a remembrance for **you** and **your** folk. You will be asked.

43:45 (Revealed in Jerusalem): Ask ones whom We sent before **you**, (Muhammad), of Our Messengers: Made We gods other than the Merciful to be worshiped?

43:87 If **you**, (Muhammad), had asked them: Who created them? They would, certainly, say: God. Then, how are they misled?

64. CHAPTER 44: THE SMOKE (AL-DUKHAN)

44:2-44:6: By the clear Book. Truly We sent it forth on a blessed night. Truly We had been ones who warn. Every wise clear command is in it, a command from Us. Truly, We had been ones who send it as a mercy from **your** Lord.

44:10 Then, **you**, (Muhammad), watch for a Day when the heavens will bring a clear smoke.

44:57 a grace from **your** Lord. That, it is the winning the sublime triumph!

44:58 Truly, We made this easy in **your** language so that perhaps they will recollect.

44:59 So **you** watch, (Muhammad)! Truly, they are ones who watch.

65. CHAPTER 45: THE ONES WHO KNEEL (AL-JATHIYAH)

45:6 These are the signs of God We recount to **you**, (Muhammad), with The Truth. Then, in which discourse, after God and His signs, will they believe?

66. CHAPTER 46: THE CURVING SANDHILLS (AL-AHQAF)

46:29 When We turned away from **you**, (Muhammad), groups of men or jinn who listen to the Quran, when they found themselves in its presence, they said: Pay heed. When it was finished, they turned to their folk, ones who warn.

67. CHAPTER 51: THE WINNOWING WINDS (AL-DHARIYAT)

51:54 So turn **you**, (Muhammad), away from them that **you** not be one who is reproached.

68. CHAPTER 88: THE OVERWHELMING EVENT (AL-GHASHIYAH)

88:1 Approached **you**, (Muhammad), the discourse of the Overwhelming Event?

> Faces on that Day will be ones that are humbled, ones that work and ones that are fatigued. They will be in a hot fire. They will be given to drink of a boiling spring. Is it not that there is no food for them but a thorny fruit. It will not fatten nor will it avail hunger. Faces on that Day will be ones that are pleasant, ones who are well-pleased by their endeavor in a magnificent Garden. They will hear no babble in it. In it is a running spring. In it are exalted couches and goblets that are set down and cushions arrayed and rugs dispersed.

88:21 Then, remind, for **you**, (Muhammad), are only one who reminds.

88:22 **You**, (Muhammad), are not over them one who is a register of their deeds.

69. CHAPTER 18: THE CAVE (AL-KAHF)

18:4-18:6: They (those who said that God has taken to Himself a son) have no knowledge about it nor had their fathers. Troublesome is a word that goes forth from their mouths. They say nothing but a lie so that perhaps **you**, (Muhammad), will be one who consumes **your**self with grief for their sake if they believe not in this discourse out of bitterness.

18:9 Have **you**, (Muhammad), assumed that the Companions of the Cave and the Bearers of Inscription had been a wonder among Our signs?

18:13 We relate this tiding (of the Companions of the Cave) to **you**, (Muhammad), with The Truth. Truly, they were male spiritual warriors who believed in their Lord and We increased them in guidance.

18:17 **You**, (Muhammad), would have seen the sun when it came up. It inclines from their cave towards the right and when it began to set, it passed them towards the left while they were in a fissure. That is of the signs of God. He whom God guides, he is one who is truly guided. He whom He causes to go astray, **you** will never find for him a protector or one who will show him the way.

18:18 **You**, (Muhammad), would assume them to be awake while they are ones who are sleeping. We turn them around and around towards the right and towards the left and their dog, one who stretches out its paws at the threshold. If **you** were to peruse them, **you** would have turned from them, running away, and would, certainly, be filled with alarm of them.

18:23-18:24: Say not about anything: Truly, I will be one who does that tomorrow, but add: If God wills. Remember **your** Lord when **you**, (Muhammad), had forgotten. Say: Perhaps my Lord will guide **me** nearer to right mindedness than this.

18:27 Recount what was revealed to **you**, (Muhammad), from the Book of **Your** Lord. There is no one who changes His Words. **You** will never find other than Him, that which is a haven.

18:46 Wealth and children are the adornment of this present life. But that which endures are ones in accord with morality. These are better with **your** Lord in reward for good deeds and better for hopefulness.

18:47 On a Day We will set in motion the mountains and **you**, (Muhammad), will see the earth as that which will depart. We will assemble them and not leave out anyone of them.

18:48 They were presented before **your** Lord ranged in rows: Certainly, you (the ungrateful) drew near Us as We created you the first time. Nay! You claimed that We never assigned for you something that is promised.

18:49 The Book was set in place and **you**, (Muhammad), will see the ones who sin being ones who are apprehensive as to what is in it. They will say: Woe to us! What is this Book? It neither leaves out anything small or great, but counted everything. They will find present what their hands had done. **Your** Lord does not wrong anyone.

18:57 Who does greater wrong than he who was reminded of the signs of his Lord, then, turned aside from them and forgot what his hands put forward? Truly, We laid sheathes on their hearts so that they should not understand it and heaviness in their ears. If **you**, (Muhammad), have called them to the guidance, yet they will not be truly guided ever.

18:58 **Your** Lord is Forgiving, Possessor of Mercy. If He were to take them to task for what they earned, He will quicken the punishment for them. But for them is what they are promised, from which they will never find a way to elude it.

70. CHAPTER 16: THE BEE (AL-NAHL)

16:14 He it is Who caused the sea to be subservient to you so that you eat from it succulent flesh and pull out of it glitter to wear and **you**, (Muhammad), see the boats, ones that plow through the waves, that you be looking for His grace and so that perhaps you will give thanks.

16:33 Look they not on but that the angels approach them or the command of **your** Lord approach? Thus, accomplished those before them. God did not wrong them. Rather, they had been doing wrong to themselves.

16:37 If **you**, (Muhammad), be eager for their guidance, then, truly, God will not guide whom He causes to go astray. They will have no ones who help.

16:43 We sent not before **you**, (Muhammad), but men to whom We reveal revelation. So ask the People of Remembrance if you had not been knowing.

16:44 With the clear portents and the ancient scrolls, We caused to descend the Remembrance to **you**, (Muhammad), that **you** will make manifest to humanity what was sent down to them so that perhaps they will reflect.

16:47 Or that He take them, destroying them little by little? Truly, **your** Lord is Gentle, Compassionate.

16:63 By God! We, certainly, sent Messengers to communities before **you**, (Muhammad). Satan made their actions appear pleasing to them. So he is their protector on this Day. Theirs will be a painful punishment.

16:64 We caused the Book to descend to **you**, (Muhammad), but that **you** will make manifest to them those things in which they were at variance in it and as a guidance and a mercy for a folk who believe.

16:68 **Your** Lord revealed to **you**, (Muhammad), the bee: Take to **your**self houses from the mountains and in the trees and in what they construct.

16:69 Again, eat of all the fruits and insert **your**self submissively into the ways of **your** Lord. Drink goes forth from their bellies in varying hues wherein is healing for humanity. Truly, in this is, certainly, a sign for a folk who reflect.

16:82 Then, if they turned away, for **you**, (Muhammad), is only the delivering of the clear message.

16:89 On the Day We raise up in every community a witness against them from among themselves and We will bring **you**, (Muhammad), about as a witness against these. We sent down to **you** the Book as an exposition that makes everything clear and as a guidance and as a mercy and as good tidings for the ones who submit to God.

16:98 So when **you**, (Muhammad), had recited the Quran, seek refuge with God from the accursed Satan.

16:101 When We substituted a sign in place of another sign—and God is greater in knowledge of what He sends down—they said: **You**, (Muhammad), are only one who devises! But most of them know not.

16:102 Say: The hallowed Spirit sent it down from **your** Lord with The Truth to make firm those who believed and as a guidance and good tidings to the ones who submit to God.

16:110 Again, truly, **your** Lord, for those who emigrated after they were persecuted and, again, struggled and endured patiently. Truly, after that, **your** Lord is Forgiving, Compassionate.

16:118 We forbade those who became Jews what We related to **you**, (Muhammad), before and We did not wrong them, except they had been doing wrong to themselves.

16:119 Again, truly, **your** Lord—to those who did evil in ignorance, again, repented after that and made things right—truly, **your** Lord after that is Forgiving, Compassionate.

16:123 Again, we revealed to **you**, (Muhammad), that **you** follow the creed of Abraham—a monotheist. He had not been among the ones who are polytheists.

16:124 Truly, the Sabbath was made for those who are at variance about it. Truly, **your** Lord will give judgment between them on the Day of Resurrection about what they had been at variance in it.

16:125 Call **you**, (Muhammad), to the way of **your** Lord with wisdom and fairer admonishment. Dispute with them in a way that is fairer. Truly, **your** Lord is He Who is greater in knowledge of whoever went astray from His way. He is greater in knowledge of the ones who are truly guided.

72. CHAPTER 14: ABRAHAM (IBRAHIM)

14:1 This is a Book We caused to descend to **you**, (Muhammad), so that **you** have brought humanity out from the shadows into the light with the permission of their Lord to the path of The Almighty, The Worthy of Praise.

14:19 Have **you**, (Muhammad), not considered that God created the heavens and the earth in Truth? If He wills, He will cause you to be put away and bring a new creation.

14:24 Have **you**, (Muhammad), not considered how God propounded a parable? What is like a good word is what is like a good tree. Its root is one that is firm and its branches are in heaven.

14:49-14:51 **You**, (Muhammad), will consider the ones who sin that Day, ones who are bound in chains. Their tunics are made of pitch and the fire will overcome their faces so that God may give recompense to every soul for what it has earned. Truly God is Swift in reckoning.

73. CHAPTER 21: THE PROPHETS (AL-ANBIYA)

21:7 We sent not before **you**, (Muhammad), but men to whom We revealed. So (you who are ungrateful) ask the People of the Remembrance if you had not been knowing.

21:25 We sent not before **you**, (Muhammad), any Messenger, but We reveal to him that there is no god but I, so worship Me.

21:34 We assigned not to any mortal before **you**, (Muhammad), immortality. If **you** were to die, will they be ones who dwell forever?

21:36 When those who were ungrateful saw **you**, (Muhammad), they mock **you** (saying): Ha! Is this he who mentions your gods? (Response): They are ones who are ungrateful for Remembrance of The Merciful.

21:41 Certainly, Messengers were ridiculed before **you**, (Muhammad). Then, those who derided them were surrounded by what they had been ridiculing.

21:46 If a breath afflicted them of punishment of **your** Lord, they would, surely, say: O woe to us! Truly, we had been ones who are unjust.

74. CHAPTER 23: THE BELIEVERS (AL-MUMINUN)

23:95 Truly, We cause **you**, (Muhammad), to see what We promise them as certainly ones who have power.

23:96 Drive **you**, (Muhammad), back evil deeds with what is fairer. We are greater in knowledge of what they allege.

75. CHAPTER 32: THE PROSTRATION (AL-SAJDAH)

32:3 Or they say: He devised it. Nay! It is The Truth from **your** Lord that **you**, (Muhammad), warn a folk to whom no warner approached them before **you**, so that perhaps they will be truly guided.

32:12 If **you**, (Muhammad), but see when the ones who sin become ones who bend down their heads before their Lord: Our Lord! We perceived and heard. So return us. We will do as ones in accord with morality. Truly, we are now ones who are certain.

32:25 Truly, **your** Lord is He Who will distinguish among them on the Day of Resurrection about what they had been at variance in it.

32:30 So turn **you**, (Muhammad), aside from them and wait awhile. Truly they are ones who are waiting awhile.

76. CHAPTER 52: THE MOUNT (AL-TUR)

52:29 So remind! **You**, (Muhammad), are not, by the divine blessing of **your** Lord, a soothsayer nor one who is possessed.

52:37 Or are the treasures of **your** Lord with them? Or are they ones who are registrars?

52:40 Or have **you**, (Muhammad), asked them for a compensation so that they are ones who will be weighed down from something owed?

52:48 So have **you**, (Muhammad), patience for the determination of **your** Lord, for, truly, **you** are under Our eyes. Glorify the praises of **your** Lord when **you** have stood up at the time of dawn.

77. CHAPTER 67: THE DOMINION (AL-MULK)

67:3 Who created the seven heavens one on another? **You**, (Muhammad), have not seen any imperfection in the creation of The Merciful. Then, return **your** sight! Have **you** seen any flaw?

67:4 Again, return **your** sight twice again and **your** sight will turn about to **you**, one that is dazzled while it is weary.

78. CHAPTER 69: THE REALITY (AL-HAQQAH)

69:17 The angels will be at its borders. The Throne of **your** Lord above them will be carried by eight on that Day.

69:52 So glorify the Name of **your** Lord, The Sublime (*al-azim*).

79. CHAPTER 70: THE STAIRWAYS OF ASCENT (AL-MAARIJ)

70:5 So have **you**, (Muhammad), patience with a graceful patience.

70:36 What is with those who were ungrateful—ones who run forward towards **you**, (Muhammad), eyes fixed in horror.

80. Chapter 78: The Tiding (al-Naba)

78:35-78:37 No idle talk will they hear in it nor any denial, a recompense from **your** Lord, a gift, a reckoning from the Lord of the heavens and the earth and of whatever is between them, The Merciful, against whom they possess no argument, a recompense from **your** Lord, a gift, a reckoning.

81. Chapter 79: The Ones Who Tear Out (al-Naziat)

79:42 They ask **you**, (Muhammad), about the Hour. When will it berth?
79:43 Then, what are **you**, (Muhammad), about that **you** remind of it?
79:44 To **your** Lord is the Utmost Boundary of it.
79:45 **You**, (Muhammad), are only one who warns to such a one whoever dreads it.

84. Chapter 30: The Romans (al-Rum)

30:30 So set **your** face towards a way of life as a monotheist. It is the nature originated by God in which He originated humanity. There is no substitution for the creation of God. That is the truth-loving way of life, but most of humanity knows not.

30:43 So set **your** face to the truth-loving way of life before that Day approaches from God and there is no turning back. They will be split up on that Day.

30:47 Certainly, We sent Messengers before **you**, (Muhammad), to their own folk. They drew near them with the clear portents. Then, We requited those who sinned. It had been an obligation on Us to help ones who believe.

30:48 God is He Who sends the winds so they raise clouds. He extends them in the heaven how He wills and He makes them into pieces until **you**, (Muhammad), sees rain drops go forth from their midst. That is when He lit it on whomever He wills of His servants. That is when they rejoice at the good tidings.

30:52 Then, truly, **you**, (Muhammad), will not cause the dead to hear nor will **you** cause the unwilling to hear, to hear the calling to them when they turned as ones who draw back.

30:53 **You**, (Muhammad), are not one who guides the unwilling to see from their fallacy. **You** have caused none to hear but those who believe in Our signs. They are ones who submit to God.

30:58 Certainly, We propounded for humanity in this, the Quran, every kind of parable. But if **you**, (Muhammad), were to bring about any sign to them, certainly, they who were ungrateful would say: Truly, you are nothing but ones who deal in falsehood.

30:60 So have **you**, (Muhammad), patience. Truly, the promise of God
is True. And let them not irritate **you**, those who are not certain in belief.

85. CHAPTER 29: THE SPIDER (AL-ANKABUT)

29:45 Recount what was revealed to **you**, (Muhammad), of the Book
and perform the formal prayer. Truly, the formal prayer prohibits depravity
and that which is unlawful, and, truly, the remembrance of God is greater.
God knows what you craft.

29:47 Thus, We caused the Book to descend to **you**, (Muhammad).
Those to whom We gave the Book before will believe in it. Of these, the people of Makkah, there are some who believe in it. None negates Our signs but
the ones who are ungrateful.

29:48 Neither had **you**, (Muhammad), been recounting from any Book
before it nor wrote **you** it with **your** right hand, for then, certainly, they would
have been in doubt, the ones who deal in falsehood.

29:51 Suffices for them not that We caused the Book to descend to **you**,
(Muhammad), which is recounted to them? Truly, in that is a mercy and a reminder for a folk who believe.

29:53 They seek **you**, (Muhammad), to hasten the punishment! Were it
not for a term, that which is determined, the punishment would have drawn
near them. Certainly, it will approach them suddenly while they are not
aware.

29:61 If **you**, (Muhammad), had asked them: Who created the heavens
and the earth and caused the sun and the moon to be subservient? They will,
certainly, say: God. Then, how they are misled!

29:63 If **you** had asked them (the ungrateful): Who sent down water from
heaven and gave life by it to the earth after its death, certainly, they would
say: God! Say: The Praise belongs to God! Nay! Most of them are not reasonable.

86. CHAPTER 83: THE ONES WHO GIVE SHORT MEASURE
(AL-MUTAFFIFIN)

83:7-83:8: Truly, the Book of the ones who act immorally is in Sijjin.
What will cause **you**, (Muhammad), to recognize what Sijjin is?
It is a written book. Woe on that Day to the ones who deny, the ones
who deny the Day of Judgment!

83:18-83:19: Truly, the book of the pious is in Illiyyun. What will cause
you, (Muhammad), to recognize what Illiyyun is?
It is a written book. Bearing witness to it are the ones who are brought
near to God.

83:24 **You**, (Muhammad), will recognize on their faces the radiancy of
bliss.

MAKKAH SIGNS IN MADINAH CHAPTERS

88. CHAPTER 8: THE SPOILS OF WAR (AL-ANFAL)

8:30 Makkah: Mention when those who were ungrateful plan against **you**, (Muhammad), to bring **you** to a standstill or to kill **you** or to drive **you** out. They plan and God plans, but God is Best of the ones who plan.

8:33 Makkah: But God had not been punishing them with **you**, (Muhammad), among them. Nor had God been One Who Punishes them while they ask for forgiveness.

MADINAH CHAPTERS

87. CHAPTER 2: THE COW (AL-BAQARAH)

2:4 Perform the formal prayer and they spend out of what We provided them, and those who believe in what was caused to descend to **you**, (Muhammad), and what was caused to descend before **you**, and they are certain of the world to come.

2:6 Truly, as for those who were ungrateful, it is the same to them whether **you**, (Muhammad), had warned them or **you** have warned them not. They believe not.

2:30 When **your** Lord said to the angels: Truly, I am assigning on the earth a viceregent. They (the angels) said: Will **You** be One Who Makes on it someone who makes corruption on it and sheds blood, while we glorify **Your** praise and sanctify **You**? He said: Truly, I know what you know not!

2:97 Say: Whoever had been an enemy of Gabriel knows, then, truly, it was sent down through him to **your** heart with the permission of God, that which establishes as true what was before it, and as a guidance and good tidings for the ones who believe.

2:99 Certainly, We caused to descend to **you**, (Muhammad), signs, clear portents. None are ungrateful for them, but the ones who disobey.

2:106 For whatever sign We nullify or cause it to be forgotten, We bring better than it, or similar to it. Have **you**, (Muhammad), not known that God is Powerful over everything?

2:107 Have **you**, (Muhammad), not known that God, to Him is the dominion of the heavens and the earth, and not for you other than God is there either a protector or a helper?

2:119 Truly, We sent **you**, (Muhammad), with The Truth as a bearer of good tidings and as a warner. **You** will not be asked about the Companions of Hellfire.

2:120 The Jews will never be well-pleased with **you**, (Muhammad), nor the Christians until **you** have followed their creed. Say: Truly, guidance of

God. It is the guidance. If **you** had followed their desires after what drew near **you** of the knowledge, there is not for **you** from God either a protector or a helper.

2:143 Thus, We made you a middle community that you be witnesses to humanity, and that the Messenger be a witness to you. We made not the direction of the formal prayer which **you** had been towards but that We make evident whoever follows the Messenger from him who turns about on his two heels. Truly, it had been grave, but for those whom God guided. God had not been wasting your belief. Truly, God is Gentle toward humanity, Compassionate.

2:144 Surely, We see the going to and fro of **your** face toward heaven. Then, We will turn **you**, (Muhammad), to a direction of formal prayer that **you** will be well pleased with it. Then, turn **your** face to the direction of the Masjid al-Haram. Wherever you had been, turn your faces to its direction. Truly, those who were given the Book know that it is The Truth from their Lord, and God is not One Who is Heedless of what they do.

2:145 Even if **you**, (Muhammad), were to bring to those who were given the Book every sign, they would not heed **your** direction of formal prayer. Nor are **you** one who heeds their direction of formal prayer. Nor are some of them ones who heed the direction of the other's formal prayer. If **you** had followed their desires after the knowledge brought about to **you**, then, truly, **you** would be among the ones who are unjust.

2:147 It is The Truth from **your** Lord. So be **you**, (Muhammad), not among the ones who contest.

2:149 From wherever **you**, (Muhammad), had gone forth, then, turn **your** face in the direction of the Masjid al-Haram. Truly, this is The Truth from **your** Lord, and God is not One Who is Heedless of what you do.

2:150 From wherever **you**, (Muhammad), had gone forth, then, turn **your** face to the direction of the Masjid al-Haram. Wherever you had been, then, turn your faces to the direction of it so that there be no disputation from humanity against you, but from those of them who did wrong. Dread them not, then, but dread Me. I fulfill My divine blessing on you—so that perhaps you will be truly guided—

2:186 When My servants asked **you**, (Muhammad), about Me, then, truly, I am near. I answer the call of one who calls when he will call to Me. So let them respond to Me and let them believe in Me, so that perhaps they will be on the right way.

2:189 They ask **you**, (Muhammad), about the new moons. Say: They are appointed times for humanity, and the pilgrimage to Makkah. It is not virtuous conduct that you approach houses from the back. Rather, virtuous conduct was to be Godfearing, and approach houses from their front doors. Be Godfearing of God so that perhaps you will prosper.

2:204 Among humanity is one whose sayings impress **you**, (Muhammad), about this present life and he calls to God to witness what is in his heart while he is most stubborn in altercation.

2:215 They ask **you**, (Muhammad), what they should spend. Say: Whatever you spent for good is for the ones who are your parents and the nearest kin and the orphans and the needy and the traveler of the way. Whatever good you accomplish, then, truly, God is Knowing of it.

2:217 They ask **you**, (Muhammad), about the Sacred Month and fighting in it. Say: Fighting in it is deplorable and barring from the way of God and ingratitude to Him. To bar from the Masjid al-Haram, and expelling people from it are more deplorable with God. Persecution is more deplorable than killing. They cease not to fight you until they repel you from your way of life, if they are able. Whoever of you goes back on his way of life, then, dies while he is one who is ungrateful, those, their actions were fruitless in the present and in the world to come. Those will be the Companions of the Fire. They are ones who will dwell in it forever.

2:219-2:220 They ask **you**, (Muhammad), about intoxicants and gambling. Say: In both of them there is deplorable sin and profits for humanity. Their sin is more deplorable than what is profitable. They ask **you** how much they should spend. Say: The extra. Thus, God makes manifest His signs to you so that perhaps you will reflect on the present and the world to come. They ask **you**, (Muhammad), about orphans. Say: Making things right for them is better. If you intermix with them, then they are your brothers/sisters. God knows the one who makes corruption from the one who makes things right. If God willed, He would have overburdened you. Truly, God is Almighty, Wise.

2:222 They ask **you**, (Muhammad), about menstruation. Say: It is an impurity, so withdraw from your wives during menstruation. Come not near them (f) until they cleanse themselves. Then, when they (f) cleansed themselves, approach them (f) as God commanded you. Truly, God loves the contrite and He loves the ones who cleanse themselves.

2:223 Your wives are a place of cultivation for you, so approach your cultivation whenever you willed and put forward for yourselves. Be God-fearing of God. Know that you will be one who encounters Him. Give **you**, (Muhammad), good tidings to the ones who believe.

2:243 Have **you**, (Muhammad), not considered those who went forth from their abodes while they were in the thousands being fearful of death? God said to them: Die! Again, He gave them life. Truly, God is Possessor of Grace for humanity except most of humanity gives not thanks.

2:258-259 Have **you**, (Muhammad), not considered him who argued with Abraham about his Lord because God gave him dominion? Mention when Abraham said: My Lord is He Who gives life and causes to die. He said: I give life and cause to die. Abraham said: Truly, God brings the sun from the East, so bring **you** the sun from the West! Then, he who was ungrateful was dumfounded. God guides not the unjust folk. Or like the one who passed by a town and it was one that has fallen down into ruins. He said: How will God give life to this after its death? So God caused him to die for a hundred years. Again, He raised him up. He said: How long had **you** lingered in expectation? He said: I lingered in expectation for a day or some part of a day. He said: Nay. **You** had lingered in expectation a hundred years. Then look on thy food and **your** drink. They are not spoiled. Look on **your** donkey. We made **you** a sign for humanity. Look on the bones, how We set them up. Again, We will clothe them with flesh. So when it became clear to him, he said: I know that God is Powerful over everything.

2:272 Their guidance is not on **you**, (Muhammad). But God guides whomever He wills. Whatever of good you spend, it is for yourselves. Spend not but looking for the Countenance of God. Whatever of good you spend, your account will be paid to you in full and you will not be wronged.

2:273 Spend for the poor, those who were restrained in the way of God and are not able to travel on the earth. The one who is ignorant assumes them to be rich because of their having reserve. **You**, (Muhammad), will recognize them by their mark. They ask not persistently of humanity. Whatever of good you spend, then, truly, God is Knowing of that.

88. Chapter 8: The Spoils of War (al-Anfal)

8:1 They ask **you**, (Muhammad), about the spoils of war. Say: The spoils of war belong to God and the Messenger so be Godfearing of God and make things right among you and obey God and his Messenger if you had been ones who believe.

8:5 Even though **your** Lord brought **you**, (Muhammad), out from **your** house with The Truth, truly, a group of people among the ones who believe were the ones who dislike it.

8:6 They dispute with **you** about The Truth—after it became clear—as if they had been driven to death and they look on at it.

8:12 Mention when **your** Lord reveals to the angels: I am, truly, with you, so make those who believed firm. I will cast alarm into the hearts of those who were ungrateful. So strike above their necks and strike each of their fingers from them.

8:17 Then, you kill them not, but God killed them. **You**, (Muhammad), had not thrown when **you** had thrown but God threw. He tries by experiment the ones who believe with a fairer trial from Him. Truly, God is Hearing, Knowing.

8:43 Mention when God causes **you**, (Muhammad), to see them as few in **your** slumbering. If He caused **you** to see them as many, you would have lost heart and contended with one another about the command except God saved you. Truly, He is Knowing of what is in the breasts.

8:50 If **you**, (Muhammad), would see when those who were ungrateful are called to themselves by the angels, they are striking their faces and their backs saying: Experience the punishment of the burning.

8:56 Those with whom **you**, (Muhammad), have made a contract, again, they break their compact every time and they are not Godfearing.

8:57 So if **you**, (Muhammad), have come upon them in war, then, break them up, whoever is behind them, so that perhaps they will recollect.

8:58 If **you**, (Muhammad), fear treachery from a folk, then, dissolve the relationship with them equally. Truly, God loves not the ones who are traitors.

8:59 Assume **you** not, (Muhammad), that those who were ungrateful will outdo Me. Truly, they will never weaken Him.

8:61 If they tended towards peace, then, tend **you**, (Muhammad), towards it and put **your** trust in God. Truly, He is The Hearing, The Knowing.

8:62 If they want to deceive **you**, (Muhammad), then, truly, God is Enough. It is He Who confirmed **you** with His help and with the ones who believe.

8:63 He brought their hearts together. If **you**, (Muhammad), had spent all that is in and on the earth, **you** would not have brought together their hearts, except God brought them together. Truly, He is Almighty, Wise.

8:64 O Prophet! God is Enough for **you** and for whoever followed **you** among the ones who believe.

8:71 But if they want treachery against **you**, (Muhammad), they, surely, betrayed God before, so He gave **you** power over them. God is Knowing, Wise.

89. Chapter 3: The Family of Imran (Al-i Imran)

3:3 He sent down to **you**, (Muhammad), the Book with The Truth, that which establishes as true what was before it. He caused to descend the Torah and the Gospel.

3:7 It is He who caused the Book to descend to **you**, (Muhammad). In it are signs, ones that are definitive. They are the essence of the Book and others, ones that are unspecific. Then, those whose hearts are swerving, they follow what was unspecific in it, looking for dissent and looking for an interpretation, but none knows its interpretation but God. The ones who are firmly rooted in knowledge say: We believed in it as all is from our Lord. And none recollects, but those imbued with intuition.

3:20 So if they argued with **you**, (Muhammad), then say: I submitted my face to God as have those who followed me. Say to those who were given the Book and to the unlettered: Have you submitted to God? If they submitted to God, then, surely, they were truly guided. If they turned away, then, on **you** is only delivering the message. God is Seeing of His servants.

3:21 Truly, those who are ungrateful for the signs of God and kill the Prophets without right and kill those who command to equity from among humanity, then, give **you**, (Muhammad), to them the tidings of a painful punishment.

3:23 Have **you**, (Muhammad), not considered those who were given a share of the Book? They are called to the Book of God to give judgment between them. Again, a group of people among them turn away and they, they are ones who turn aside.

3:58 These We recount to **you**, (Muhammad), are of the signs and the wise remembrance.

3:60 The Truth is from **your** Lord, so be not of the ones who contest.

3:61 Then, to whoever argued with **you**, (Muhammad), about it after what drew near **you** of the knowledge, say: Approach now! Let us call to our children and your children and our women and your women and ourselves and yourselves. Again we will humbly supplicate, and we lay the curse of God on the ones who lie.

3:75 Among the People of the Book is he who, if **you**, (Muhammad), have entrusted him with a hundredweight, he would give it back to **you**. Among them is he who, if **you** have entrusted him with a dinar, he would not give it back to **you** unless **you** had continued as one who stands over him. That is because they said: There is no way of moral duty on us as to the unlettered. They are lying against God while they, they know.

3:108 These are the signs of God. We recount them to **you**, (Muhammad), in Truth. God wants not injustice in the worlds.

3:121 When **you**, (Muhammad), had set forth in the early morning from **your** family to place the ones who believe at their positions for fighting, God is Hearing, Knowing.

3:124 Mention when **you**, (Muhammad), have said to the ones who believe: Suffices you not that your Lord will reinforce you with three thousand among the angels? Ones who are caused to descend,

3:128 It is none of **your** affair at all if He turns to them in forgiveness or He punishes them, for, truly, they are ones who are unjust.

3:154 Again, He caused to descend safety for you after lament. Sleepiness overcomes a section of you while a section caused themselves grief thinking of God without right, a thought out of the Age of Ignorance. They say: Have we any part in the command? Say: Truly, the command is entirely from God. They conceal within themselves what they show not to **you**, (Muhammad). They say: If there had been for us any part in the command, we would not be killed here. Say: Even if you had been in your houses, those would have departed—whom it was prescribed they be slain—for the Final Place of sleeping, so that God tests what is in your breasts and He proves what is in your hearts. God is Knowing of what is in the breasts.

3:159 It is by the mercy of God **you**, (Muhammad), were gentle with them. If **you** had been hard, harsh of heart, they would have broken away from around **you**. So pardon them and ask for forgiveness for them. Take counsel with them in the affair. But when **you** are resolved, then, put **your** trust in God. Truly, God loves the ones who put their trust in Him.

3:176 Let not those who compete with one another in ingratitude dishearten **you**, (Muhammad). Truly, they will never injure God at all. God wants to assign no allotment for them in the world to come and for them is a tremendous punishment.

3:184 Then if they denied **you**, (Muhammad), surely, Messengers before **you** were denied who drew near with the clear portents and the Psalms and the illuminating Book.

3:196 Let not the going to and fro delude **you**, (Muhammad), of those who were ungrateful in the land

90. CHAPTER 33: THE CONFEDERATES (AL-AHZAB)

33:2 Follow what is revealed to **you**, (Muhammad), from **your** Lord. Truly, God is Aware of what you had been doing.

33:3 Put **your** trust in God. God sufficed as a Trustee.

33:6 The Prophet is nearer by to ones who believe than their own souls. His wives are their mothers. Those who are blood relations, some of them are nearer to each other in what is prescribed by God than the other ones who believe and ones who emigrate, but accomplish what you may for your protectors as ones who are honorable. This has been inscribed in the Book.

33:19 Then, when fear drew near, **you**, (Muhammad), will see them looking on **you**, their eyes rolling like he who is overcome by death. But when their fear went, they abused you with sharp tongues in their covetousness for good things. Those believe not. God caused their actions to fail. That had been easy for God.

33:28 O Prophet! Say to **your** spouses: If you had been wanting this present life and its adornment, then, approach now. I will give you enjoyment and set you (f) free, releasing gracefully.

33:37 Mention when **you**, (Muhammad), say to him to whom God was gracious and to whom **you** were gracious: Hold back **your** spouse to **your**self and be Godfearing of God. But **you** conceal in **your**self what God is One Who Shows and **you** dread humanity whereas God has a better right that **you** dread Him. So when Zayd satisfied the necessary formality, We gave her to **you** in marriage so that there be no fault for ones who believe in respect of the spouses of their adopted sons when they (m) satisfied the necessary formality. The command of God had been one that is accomplished.

33:45 O Prophet! Truly, We sent **you**, (Muhammad), as one who bears witness and as one who gives good tidings and as a warner.

33:48 Obey not the ones who are ungrateful and the ones who are hypocrites and heed not their annoyance and put **your** trust in God. God sufficed as a Trustee.

33:50 O Prophet! Truly, We have permitted to **you**, (Muhammad), **your** spouses (f), those whom **you** had given their (f) compensation and whom **your** right hand possessed from that God gave **you** as spoils of war and the daughters of **your** paternal uncles and the daughters of **your** paternal aunts and the daughters of **your** maternal uncles and the daughters of **your** maternal aunts those who emigrated with **you** and a woman, one who believes, if she bestowed herself on the Prophet. If the Prophet wanted to take her in marriage—that is exclusively for **you**—not for the other ones who believe. Surely, We know what We imposed on them about their spouses and whom their right hands possessed (f) that there be no fault on **you**. God had been Forgiving, Compassionate.

33:51 **You**, (Muhammad), will put off whom **you** will of them (f) and **you** will give refuge to whom **you** will. Whomever **you** will be looking for of whom **you** had set aside, there is no blame on **you** to receive her again. That is likelier that will be refreshed their (f) eyes and they (f) not feel remorse and may they (f) be well-pleased with what **you** had given them (f), all of them (f). God knows what is in your hearts. God had been Knowing, Forbearing.

33:52 Women are not lawful for **you**, (Muhammad), in marriage after this, nor that **you** were taking them (f) in exchange for other spouses, even though their (f) goodness impressed **you**, but whom **your** right hand possessed (f). God had been watching over everything.

33:59 O Prophet! Say to **your** spouses (f) and **your** daughters and the females, ones who believe to draw closer their (f) outer garments over themselves (f). That is more fitting so that they (f) be recognized and not be maligned. God had been Forgiving, Compassionate.

33:60 If the ones who are hypocrites refrain not themselves and those who in their hearts is a sickness and the ones who make a commotion in the city, We will stir **you**, (Muhammad), up against them. Again, they will not be **your** neighbors in it, but a little while.

33:62 This is a custom of God with those who passed away before. **You**, (Muhammad), will never find in a custom of God any substitution.

33:63 Humanity asks **you**, (Muhammad), about the Hour. Say: The knowledge of it is only with God. What will cause **you** to recognize that perhaps the Hour be near?

91. CHAPTER 60: SHE WHO IS PUT TO A TEST (AL-MUMTAHINAH)

60:12 O Prophet! When drew near **you** the females, ones who are believers, to take the pledge of allegiance to **you** that they will ascribe nothing as partners with God nor will they steal nor will they commit adultery nor will they kill their children, nor will they approach making false charges to harm another's reputation that they devise between their (f) hands and their (f) feet, and that they rebel not against **you** in anything that is honorable.

Then, take their (f) pledge of allegiance and ask forgiveness from God for them (f). Truly, God is Forgiving, Compassionate.

92. Chapter 4: The Women (al-Nisa)

4:41 Then, how will it be when We brought about from each community a witness and We brought **you** about as witness against these?

4:44 Have **you**, (Muhammad), not considered those who were given a share of the Book? They exchange fallacy and they want you to go astray from the way.

4:46 Among those who became Jews are those who tamper with words out of context. They say: We heard and we rebelled and: Hear—without being one who is caused to hear and: Look at us—distorting their tongues and discrediting the way of life. If they had said: We heard and we obeyed and: Hear **you**, (Muhammad), and: Wait for us, it would have been better for them and more upright, except God cursed them for their ingratitude. So they believe not but a few.

4:49 Have **you**, (Muhammad), not considered those who make themselves seem pure? Nay! God makes pure whom He wills and they will not be wronged in the least.

4:51 Have **you**, (Muhammad), not considered those who were given a share of the Book? They believe in false gods and false deities and they say to those who were ungrateful: These are better guided than those who believed in the way!

4:52 Those are those whom God cursed. For whomever God curses, then, **you**, (Muhammad), will not find a helper for him.

4:60 Have **you**, (Muhammad), not considered those who claim that they believed in what was caused to descend to **you** and what was caused to descend before **you**? They want to take their disputes to another for judgment—to false deities—while they were commanded to disbelieve in them, but Satan wants to cause them to go astray—a far wandering astray.

4:61 When it was said to them: Approach now to what God caused to descend and approach now to the Messenger, **you** had seen the ones who are hypocrites barring **you** with hindrances.

4:62 How then will it be when they are lit on by an affliction for what their hands put forward? Again, they drew near **you**, (Muhammad), swearing by God: Truly, we wanted but kindness and conciliation!

4:64 We never sent a Messenger, but he is obeyed with the permission of God. If, when they did wrong themselves, they drew near to **you**, (Muhammad), and asked for the forgiveness of God and the Messenger asked for forgiveness for them, they found God Accepter of Repentance, Compassionate.

4:65 But no! By **your** Lord! They will not believe until they make **you**, (Muhammad), a judge in what they disagreed about between them. Again, they find within themselves no impediment to what **you** had decided, resigning themselves to submission, full submission.

4:77 Have **you**, (Muhammad), not considered those who when it was said to them: Limit your hands from warfare and perform the formal prayer and give the purifying alms? Then, when fighting was prescribed for them, there was a group of people among them who dread humanity, even dreading God or with a more severe dreading, and they said: Our Lord! Why had **You** prescribed fighting for us? Why had **You** not postponed it for another near term for us? Say, (Muhammad): The enjoyment of the present is little and the world to come is better. For whomever was Godfearing, you will not be wronged in the least.

4:78 Wherever you be, death will overtake you, even if you had been in imposing towers. When benevolence lights on them, they say: This is from God. When an evil deed lights on them, they say: This is from **you**, (Muhammad). Say: All is from God. So what is with these folk that they understand almost no discourse?

4:79 Whatever of benevolence lit on **you**, (Muhammad), is from God. Whatever evil deeds lit on **you**, then, is from **your**self. We sent **you** to humanity as a Messenger. God sufficed as Witness.

4:80 Whoever obeys the Messenger, surely, obeyed God and whoever turned away, then We sent **you**, (Muhammad), not as a guardian over them.

4:81 They say: Obedience! Then, when they departed from **you**, (Muhammad), a section of them spent the night planning on other than what **you** have said. God records what they spend the night planning. So turn aside from them and put **your** trust in God. God sufficed as Trustee.

4:84 So fight **you**, (Muhammad), in the way of God. **You** are not placed with a burden but for **your**self. Encourage the ones who believe. Perhaps God will limit the might of those who were ungrateful. God is Stauncher in might and Stauncher in making an example.

4:88 Then, what is it with you that you be two factions concerning the ones who are hypocrites? And God overthrew them for what they earned? Want you to guide whom God caused to go astray? Whomever God causes to go astray, **you**, (Muhammad), will never find for him a way.

4:102 When **you**, (Muhammad), had been among them, performing the formal prayer with them, let a section of them stand up with **you** and take their weapons. When they prostrated themselves, then, let them move behind you and let another section approach who has not yet formally prayed. Then, let them formally pray with **you** and let them take their precaution and their weapons. Those who were ungrateful wished for you to be heedless of your weapons and your sustenance. They would turn against you with a single turning. There is no blame on you if you had been annoyed because of rain or you had been sick that you lay down your weapons. Take precaution for yourselves. Truly, God prepared for the ones who are ungrateful a despised punishment.

4:105 Truly, We caused to descend to **you**, (Muhammad), the Book with The Truth so that **you** will give judgment between humanity by what God caused **you** to see. Be **you** not the pleader for ones who are traitors.

4:113 Were it not for the grace of God on **you**, (Muhammad), and His mercy, a section of them was about to do something that would cause **you** to go astray. They cause none to go astray but themselves and they injure **you** not at all. God caused the Book to descend to **you** and wisdom and taught **you** what **you** are not knowing. The grace of God had been sublime upon **you**.

4:127 They ask **you**, (Muhammad), for advice about women. Say: God pronounces to you about them (f) and what is recounted to you in the Book about the orphans of women, those to whom (f) you give not what was prescribed for them (f) because you prefer that you marry them (f) and about the ones taken advantage of due to weakness among children and that you stand up for the orphans with equity. Whatever you accomplish of good, then, truly, God had been Knowing of it.

4:138 Give **you**, (Muhammad), good tidings to the ones who are hypocrites that, truly, for them is a painful punishment.

4:142-4:143: Truly, the ones who are hypocrites seek to deceive God. It is He, He is The One Who Deceives them and when they stand up for formal prayer, they stand up lazily to make display to humanity, and they are not remembering God but a little as ones who are wavering between this and that, neither with these, nor with these. Whom God causes to go astray, **you**, (Muhammad), will never find a way for him.

4:145 Truly, the ones who are hypocrites will be in the lowest, deepest reaches of the fire. **You**, (Muhammad), will not find for them any helper,

4:153 The People of the Book ask **you**, (Muhammad), that **you** have sent down to them a Book from heaven. Surely, they had asked Moses for greater than that. Then, they said: Cause us to see God publicly. So a thunderbolt took them for their injustice. Again, they took the calf to themselves after what drew near to them—the clear portents. Even so We pardoned that. We gave Moses a clear authority.

4:162 But the ones who are firmly rooted in knowledge among them and the ones who believe, they believe in what was caused to descend to **you**, (Muhammad), and what was caused to descend before **you**. They are the ones who perform the formal prayer. They are the ones who give the purifying alms. They are the ones who believe in God and the Last Day. It is those to whom We will give a sublime compensation.

4:163 Truly, We revealed to **you**, (Muhammad), as We revealed to Noah and the Prophets after him. We revealed to Abraham and Ishmael and Isaac and Jacob and the Tribes and Jesus and Job and Jonah and Aaron and Solomon. We gave David the Psalms.

4:164 Messengers We related to **you**, (Muhammad), before and Messengers We relate to **you** not. God spoke directly to Moses, speaking directly.

4:166 God bears witness to what He caused to descend to **you**, (Muhammad). He caused it to descend with His knowledge. The angels also bear witness. God sufficed as witness.

4:176 They ask **you**, (Muhammad), for advice. Say: God pronounces to you about indirect heirs. If a man perished and he be without children and he has a sister, then, for her is half of what he left. He inherits from her if she be without children. If there had been two sisters, then, for them (f), two-thirds of what he left. If there had been brothers/sisters, men and women, the man will have the like allotment as two females. God makes manifest to you so that you go not astray, and God is Knowing of everything.

94. CHAPTER 57: IRON (AL-HADID)

57:12 On a Day **you**, (Muhammad), will see the males, ones who believe and the females, ones who believe, their light coming eagerly in advance of them and on their right: Good tidings for you this Day, Gardens beneath which rivers run, ones who will dwell in them forever. That, it is the winning the sublime triumph!

57:20 Know that this present life is only a pastime, a diversion and an adornment and a mutual boasting among you and a rivalry in respect to wealth and children as the likeness of plenteous rain water. The plants impressed ones who are ungrateful. Again, it withers; then, **you**, (Muhammad), have seen it yellowing. Again, it becomes chaff while in the world to come there is severe punishment and forgiveness from God and contentment. And this present life is nothing but a delusion of enjoyment.

95. CHAPTER 47: THE CURVING SANDHILLS (AL-AHQAF)

47:13 How many a town had there been which was stronger in strength than **your** town which drove **you**, (Muhammad), out, that We have caused to perish? There was no one who helps them!

47:16 Among them are some who listen to **you**, (Muhammad), until when they went forth from **you**. They said to those who were given the knowledge: What was that he said just now? Those are those upon whose hearts God set a seal. They followed their own desires.

47:19 So know **you**, (Muhammad), that there is no god but God and ask forgiveness for **your** impieties and also for the males, ones who believe and the females, ones who believe, and God knows your place of turmoil and your place of lodging.

47:20 Those who believed say: Why was a Chapter of the Quran not caused to descend? But when was caused to descend a definitive Chapter of the Quran and fighting was remembered in it, **you**, (Muhammad), had seen those who in their hearts is a sickness looking on **you** with the look of one who is fainting at death.

47:30 If We will, We would have caused **you**, (Muhammad), to see them. **You** would have recognized them by their mark. But, certainly, **you** will recognize them by the twisting of sayings. God knows all your actions.

96. CHAPTER 13: THUNDER (AL-RAD)

13:1 That are the signs of the Book, and what were caused to descend to **you**, (Muhammad), from **your** Lord is The Truth, except most of humanity believes not.

13:5 If **you**, (Muhammad), marvel, then, wonder at their saying: When we had been earth dust, will we, truly, be in a new creation? Those are those who were ungrateful to their Lord. Those will have yokes around their necks. Those will be the Companions of the Fire. They, ones who will dwell in it forever.

13:6 They seek **you**, (Muhammad), to hasten on evil deeds before the benevolence. Surely, passed away before them exemplary punishments. But, truly, **your** Lord is certainly, The Possessor of Forgiveness for humanity in spite of their injustice. Truly, **your** Lord is Severe in repayment.

13:7 Those who were ungrateful say: Why was a sign not caused to descend to him from his Lord? **You**, (Muhammad), are only one who warns, and one who guides every folk.

13:19 Then, is he who knows what was caused to descend to **you**, (Muhammad), from **your** Lord to be The Truth like he who is unwilling to see? It is only those imbued with intuition who recollect.

13:30 Thus, We sent **you**, (Muhammad), to a community. Surely, passed away other communities before it so that **you** would recount to them what We revealed to **you** and they are ungrateful to The Merciful. Say: He is my Lord. There is no god but He. In Him I put my trust and to Him I am turning in repentance.

13:32 Certainly, Messengers were ridiculed before **you**, (Muhammad), but I granted indulgence to those who were ungrateful. Again, I took them. How had been My repayment!

13:36 Those to whom We gave the Book are glad at what was caused to descend to **you**. There are among the confederates some who reject some of it. Say: I was commanded to worship only God and not to ascribe partners with Him. I call to Him and to Him is my destination.

13:37 Thus, We caused to descend an Arabic determination. If **you**, (Muhammad), had followed their desires after what drew near **you** of the knowledge, **you** would not have against God either a protector or one who is a defender.

13:38 Certainly, We sent Messengers before **you**, (Muhammad), and We assigned for them spouses and offspring. It had not been for a Messenger to bring a sign but with the permission of God. For every term there is a Book.

13:40 Whether We cause **you**, (Muhammad), to see some of what We have promised them or call **you** to Ourselves, on **you** is delivering the message and on Us is the reckoning.

13:43 Those who were ungrateful say: **You**, (Muhammad), are not one who is sent. Say: God sufficed as a witness between me and between you and whoever has knowledge of the Book.

97. Chapter 55: The Merciful (al-Rahman)

55:27 The Countenance of **your** Lord will remain forever, Possessor of The Majesty and The Splendor.

55:78 Blessed be the Name of **your** Lord, Possessor of The Majesty and The Splendor.

98. Chapter 76: The Human Being (al-Insan)

76:19 Ones who are immortal youths will go around them whom, when **you**, (Muhammad), had seen them, **you** would assume them to be scattered pearls.

76:20 When **you**, (Muhammad), had seen them, again, **you** will have seen bliss and a great dominion.

76:23 Truly, We sent down to **you**, (Muhammad), the Quran, a sending down successively.

76:24 So have **you**, (Muhammad), patience for the determination of **your** Lord and obey not any one of them, not the ones who are perverted nor the ungrateful.

76:25 Remember **you**, (Muhammad), the Name of **your** Lord at early morning dawn and eventide.

76:26 Prostrate **your**self to Him during the night and glorify Him a lengthy part of the night.

99. Chapter 65: Divorce (al-Talaq)

65:1 O Prophet! When you divorced your wives, then, divorce them (f) after their (f) waiting periods and count their (f) waiting periods. Be God-fearing of God, your Lord. Drive them (f) not out from their (f) houses nor let them (f) go forth unless they approach a manifest indecency. These are the ordinances of God. Whoever violates the ordinances of God, then, truly, he did wrong to himself. **You**, (Muhammad), are not informed so that perhaps God will cause to evoke something after that affair.

101. Chapter 59: The Banishment (al-Hashr)

59:11 Have **you**, (Muhammad), not considered those who are ones who are hypocrites? They say to their brothers—those who were ungrateful—among the People of the Book: If you were driven out, we, certainly, will go forth with you and we will never obey anyone against you ever. If you were fought against, we will, certainly, help you. God bears witness that they, truly, are ones who lie.

59:21 If We had caused this, the Quran, to descend on a mountain, **you**, (Muhammad), would have seen it as that which is humbled, one that is split open from dreading God. There are the parables that We propound for humanity so that perhaps they will reflect.

102. Chapter 24: The Light (al-Nur)

24:41 Have **you**, (Muhammad), not considered that glorifies God whatever is in the heavens and the earth and the birds, ones standing in ranks? Each knew its formal prayer and its glorification. God is Knowing of what they accomplish.

24:43 Have **you**, (Muhammad), not considered how God propels clouds and, again, brings what is between them together? Again, He lays them into a heap. **You** have seen the rain drops go forth in the midst. He sends down from the heaven mountains of rain in which there is hail. He lights it on whom He wills and turns away from it whom He wills. The gleams of His lightning almost take away the sight.

24:53 They swore by God their most earnest oaths that if **you**, (Muhammad), would command them, they would go forth. Say: Swear not; honorable obedience is better. Truly God is Aware of what you do.

24:62 The ones who believe are only those who believe in God and His Messenger. When they had been with him on a collective matter, they go not until they asked his permission. Truly, those who ask **your** permission, those are those who believed in God and His Messenger. So when they ask **your** permission for some of their affairs, give permission to whom **you**, (Muhammad), had willed of them, and ask God for forgiveness for them. Truly, God is Forgiving, Compassionate.

103. Chapter 22: The Pilgrimage (al-Hajj)

22:2 Every one who is breast feeding will be negligent of whoever she breast fed. Every pregnant woman will bring forth a foetus and **you**, (Muhammad), will see humanity intoxicated yet they will not be intoxicated. But the punishment of God will be severe.

22:10 That is because of what **your** two hands put forward! Truly, God is not unjust to His servants.

22:18 Have **you**, (Muhammad), not considered that to God prostrates to Him whoever is in the heavens and whoever is in and on the earth and the sun and the moon and the stars, the mountains, the trees and the moving creatures, and many of humanity while there are many on whom the punishment will be realized. He whom God despises, then, there is no one who honors him. Truly, God accomplishes whatever He wills.

22:27 Announce to humanity the pilgrimage to Makkah. They will approach **you**, (Muhammad), on foot and on every thin camel. They will approach from every deep ravine

22:34 For every community We assigned devotional acts that they may remember the Name of God over what We provided them of flocks of animals. Your God is One God. Submit to Him, and give **you**, (Muhammad), good tidings to the ones who humble themselves.

22:37 Neither their flesh nor their blood attains to God, rather, God-consciousness from you attains Him. Thus, He caused them to be subservient to you that you magnify God in that He guided you. Give **you**, (Muhammad), good tidings to the ones who are doers of good.

22:42 If they deny **you**, (Muhammad), surely, the folk of Noah denied before **you** and Aad and Thamud.

22:47 Seek they that **you**, (Muhammad), hasten the punishment? God never breaks His Promise. Truly, a day with **your** Lord is as a thousand years of what you number.

22:52 We sent not before **you**, (Muhammad), any Messenger nor Prophet, but when he fantasized, Satan cast fantasies into him. But God nullifies what Satan casts. Again, God set clear His signs. God is Knowing, Wise,

22:54 Those who were given the knowledge know that it is The Truth from **your** Lord, so that they believe in it and humble their hearts to Him. Truly, God is One Who Guides those who believed to a straight path.

22:63 Have **you**, (Muhammad), not considered that God caused water to descend from heaven? Then, in the morning, the earth becomes green. Truly, God is Subtle, Aware.

22:65 Have **you**, (Muhammad), not considered that God caused to be subservient to you what is in and on the earth? And the boats run through the sea by His command. He holds back the heaven so that it not fall on the earth, but by His permission. Truly, to humanity God is Gentle, Compassionate.

22:67 For every community We assigned devotional acts so that they be ones who perform rites. So let them not bicker with **you**, (Muhammad), in the command. Call **you** to **your** Lord. Truly, **you** are on a straight guidance.

22:68 If they disputed with **you**, (Muhammad), then, **you** say: God is greater in knowledge about what you do.

22:70 Have **you**, (Muhammad), not known that God knows what is in the heaven and the earth? Truly, that is in a Book. Truly, that is easy for God.

22:72 When Our signs are recounted to them, clear portents, **you**, (Muhammad), will recognize on the faces of those who were ungrateful, that they are the ones who are rejected. They are about to rush upon those who recount Our signs to them. Say: Shall I tell you of worse than that? God promised the fire to those who were ungrateful. And miserable will be the Homecoming!

104. Chapter 63: The Hypocrites (al-Munafiqun)

63:1 When the ones who are hypocrites drew near **you**, (Muhammad), they said: We bear witness that **you** are, truly, the Messenger of God. God knows that **you** are, truly, His Messenger and God bears witness that the ones who are hypocrites are ones who lie.

63:4 When **you**, (Muhammad), have seen them, their physiques impress **you**. When they speak, **you** hear their saying. It is as if they had been propped up timber. They assume that every Cry is against them. They are the enemy so beware of them. God took the offensive. How they are misled!

63:5 When it was said to them: Approach now. The Messenger of God asks forgiveness for you. They twist their heads and **you**, (Muhammad), had seen them dissuading while they are ones who grow arrogant.

63:6 It is the same to them whether **you**, (Muhammad), had asked for forgiveness for them or **you** had not asked for forgiveness for them. God will never forgive them. Truly, God guides not the folk, the ones who disobey.

105. Chapter 58: She Who Disputes (al-Mujadilah)

58:1 Surely, God heard the saying of she who disputes with **you**, (Muhammad), about her spouse and she complains to God and God hears conversing between you both. Truly, God is Hearing, Seeing.

58:7 Have **you**, (Muhammad), not considered that God knows whatever is in the heavens and whatever is in and on the earth. There will be no conspiring secretly of three, but He is their fourth nor of five, but He is the sixth, nor of fewer than that nor of more, but He is with them wherever they had been. Again, He will tell them of what they did on the Day of Resurrection. Truly, God is Knowing of everything.

58:8 Have **you**, (Muhammad), not considered those who were prohibited from conspiring secretly? Again, they revert to what they were prohibited from and hold secret counsel in sin and deep-seated dislike and in opposition to the Messenger? When they drew near **you**, they gave **you** greetings with that with which God gives not as a greeting to **you** and they say to themselves: Why punishes us not God for what we say? Hell will be enough for them. They will roast in it. Then, miserable will be the Homecoming!

58:14 Have **you**, (Muhammad), considered those who turned in friendship to a folk against whom God was angry? They are not of you, nor are you of them and they swear to a lie while they know.

58:22 **You**, (Muhammad), will not find any folk who believe in God and the Last Day who make friends with whoever opposed God and His Messenger even if they had been their fathers or their sons or their brothers or their kinspeople. Those, He prescribed belief in their hearts, and confirmed them with a Spirit from Himself. And He will cause them to enter Gardens beneath which rivers run as ones who will dwell in them forever. God was well-pleased with them and they were well-pleased with Him. Those are the

Party of God. Lo! the Party of God. They are the ones who prosper.

106. CHAPTER 49: THE INNER APARTMENTS (AL-HUJURAT)

49:4 Truly, those who cry out to **you**, (Muhammad), from behind the inner apartments, most of them are not reasonable.

49:5 If they endured patiently until **you** would go forth to them, it would have been better for them. And God is Forgiving, Compassionate.

49:17 They show grace to **you**, (Muhammad), that they submitted to God. Say: Show you submission to God as grace to me? Nay! God shows grace to you in that He guided you to belief if you, truly, had been ones who are sincere.

107. CHAPTER 66: THE FORBIDDING (AL-TAHRIM)

66:1 O Prophet! Why have **you** forbidden what God permitted to **you,** looking for the goodwill of **your** spouses? God is Forgiving, Compassionate.

66:3 Mention when the Prophet confided to one of his spouses a discourse, she, then, told it to another. God disclosed to him of it. He acquainted her with some of it and turned aside some of it. When he told her about it, she said: Who communicated this to **you**, (Muhammad)? He said: The Knowing, The Aware told me.

66:9 O Prophet! Struggle against the ones who are ungrateful and the ones who are hypocrites and be **you**, (Muhammad), harsh against them. Their place of shelter will be hell. Miserable will be the Homecoming!

110. CHAPTER 62: THE CONGREGATION (AL-JUMUAH)

62:2 He it is Who raised up among the unlettered a Messenger, (Muhammad), from among them who recounts His signs to them and makes them pure and teaches them the Book and wisdom even though they had been before certainly, clearly going astray

62:11 When they considered a transaction or a diversion, they broke away toward it, and left **you**, (Muhammad), as one who is standing up. Say: What is with God is better than any diversion or than any transaction. God is Best of the ones who provide.

111. CHAPTER 48: THE VICTORY (AL-FATH)

48:1-48:3 Truly, We gave victory to **you**, (Muhammad), a clear victory, that God may forgive **you**, (Muhammad), what was former of **your** impiety and what will remain behind that He may fulfill His divine blessing on **you** and guide **you** on a straight path, and that God help **you**, (Muhammad), with a mighty help.

48:8 Truly, We sent **you**, (Muhammad), as one who bears witness and one who gives good tidings and as a warner,

48:10 Truly, those who take the pledge of allegiance to **you**, (Muhammad), take the pledge of alliance only to God. The hand of God is over their hands. Then, whoever broke his oath, breaks his oath only to the harm of himself. Whoever lived up to what he made as a contract with God, He will give him a sublime compensation.

48:11 The ones who are left behind will say to **you**, (Muhammad), among the nomads: Our property and our people occupied us, so ask forgiveness for us. They say with their tongues what is not in their hearts. Say: Who, then, has sway over you against God at all if He wanted to harm you or wanted to bring you profit? Nay! God had been aware of what you do.

48:12 Nay! You thought that the Messenger, (Muhammad), would never turn about and the ones who believe to their people ever, and that was made to appear pleasing in your hearts. But you thought a reprehensible thought, and you had been a lost folk.

48:18 God was well-pleased with the ones who believe (f) when they take the pledge of allegiance to **you**, (Muhammad), beneath the tree for He knew what was in their hearts and He caused the tranquility to descend on them and He repaid them with a victory near at hand.

48:23 This is the way of God which was, surely, in force before. **You**, (Muhammad), will never find in the way of God any substitution.

48:29 Muhammad is the Messenger of God. Those who are with him are severe against the one who is ungrateful, but compassionate among themselves. **You** have seen them as ones who bow down as ones who prostrate themselves. They are looking for grace from God and contentment. Their mark is on their faces from the effects of prostration. This is their parable in the Torah. Their parable in the Gospel is like sown seed that brought out its shoot, energized. It, then, became stout and rose straight on its plant stalk impressing the ones who sow so that He enrage by them the ones who are ungrateful, God promised those who believed and did as the ones in accord with morality, for them forgiveness and a sublime compensation.

112. CHAPTER 5: THE TABLE SPREAD WITH FOOD (AL-MAIDA)

5:4 They ask **you**, (Muhammad), what was permitted to them. Say: That which is good was permitted to you and what you taught of hunting creatures, as one who teaches hunting dogs of what God taught you. So eat of what they seized for you and remember the Name of God over it and be Godfearing of God. Truly, God is Swift in reckoning.

5:13 Then, for their breaking their solemn promise, We cursed them and We made their hearts ones that harden. They tamper with the words out of context and they forgot an allotment of what they were reminded of in it. **You**, (Muhammad), will not cease to peruse the treachery of them, but a few of them. Then, overlook and pardon them. Truly, God loves the ones who are doers of good.

5:40 Have **you**, (Muhammad), not known that to God, to Him belongs the dominion of the heavens and the earth? He punishes whom He wills and He forgives whom He wills. And God is Powerful over everything.

5:41 O Messenger! Let them not dishearten **you**, (Muhammad)—those who compete with one another in ingratitude among those who said: We believed with their mouths while their hearts believe not. Among those who became Jews are ones who hearken to lies, ones who hearken to folk of others who approach not **you**. They tamper with the words out of context. They say: If you were given this, then, take it, but if you are not given this, then, beware! For whomever God wants to test, **you** will never have sway over him against God at all. Those are whom God wants not to purify their hearts. For them in the present is degradation. For them in the world to come is a tremendous punishment.

5:42 They are ones who hearken to lies, the ones who devour the wrongful. Then, if they drew near **you**, (Muhammad), then, give **you** judgment between them or turn aside from them. If **you** turn aside from them, then, they will never injure **you** at all. If **you** had given judgment, then, give judgment between them with equity. Truly, God loves the ones who act justly.

5:43 How will they make **you**, (Muhammad), their judge while with them is the Torah wherein is the determination of God? Yet, again, after that, they turn away. Those are the ones who believe not.

5:48 We caused the Book to descend to **you**, (Muhammad), with The Truth, that which establishes as true what was before it of the Book and that which preserves it. So give judgment between them by what God caused to descend. Follow not their desires that drew near **you** against The Truth. For each among you We made a divine law and an open road. If God willed, He would have made you one community to try you with what He gave you so be forward in good deeds. To God is your return altogether. Then, He will tell you about what you had been at variance in it.

5:49 Give judgment between them by what God caused to descend and follow not their desires and beware of them so that they tempt **you**, (Muhammad), not from some of what God caused to descend to **you**. If they turned away, then, know that God only wants that He light on them for some of their impieties. Truly, many within humanity are ones who disobey.

5:52 **You**, (Muhammad), see those who in their hearts is a sickness. They compete with one another. They say: We dread that a turn of fortune should light on us. Then, perhaps God brings a victory or a command from Him? Then, they will become—from what they kept secret within themselves— ones who are remorseful.

5:60 Say: Will I tell **you**, (Muhammad), of worse than that as a reward from God? He whom God cursed and with whom He was angry and He made some of them into apes and swine who worshiped the false deities. Those are worse placed and ones who go astray from the right way.

5:62 **You** see many of them competing with one another in sin and deep seated dislike and in consuming the wrongful. What they had been doing was miserable.

5:64 The Jews said: The hand of God is one that is restricted! Restricted were their hands! They were cursed for what they said. Nay! His hands are ones that are stretched out: He spends how He wills. Certainly, many of them increase by what was caused to descend to **you**, (Muhammad), from **your** Lord in defiance and in ingratitude. We cast among them enmity and hatred until the Day of Resurrection. Whenever they kindled a fire of war, God extinguished it. And they hasten about corrupting in and on the earth. And God loves not the ones who make corruption.

5:67 O Messenger! State what was caused to descend to **you**, (Muhammad), from **your** Lord, for if **you** have not accomplished it, then, **you** will not have stated His message. God will save **you** from the harm of humanity. Truly, God guides not the folk, the ones who are ungrateful.

5:68 Say: O People of the Book! You are not based on anything until you adhere to the Torah and the Gospel and what was caused to descend to you from your Lord. Certainly, many of them increase by what was caused to descend to **you**, (Muhammad), from **your** Lord in defiance and ingratitude. So grieve not for folk, the ones who are ungrateful.

5:80 **You**, (Muhammad), have seen many of them turning away to those who were ungrateful. Miserable was what was put forward for them themselves so that God was displeased with them and in their punishment they are ones who will dwell in it forever.

5:82 Truly, **you**, (Muhammad), will find the hardest of humanity in enmity to those who believed are the Jews and those who have ascribed partners with God. Certainly, **you** will find the nearest of them in affection to those who believed are those who said: We are Christians. That is because among them are priests and monks and they grow not arrogant.

5:83 When they heard what was caused to descend to the Messenger, **you**, (Muhammad), see their eyes overflow with tears because they recognized The Truth. They say: Our Lord! We believed so write us down with the ones who bear witness.

5:100 Say: Not on the same level are the bad and what is good even if the prevalence of the bad impressed **you**, (Muhammad). So be Godfearing of God, O those imbued with intuition, so that perhaps you will prosper.

113. CHAPTER 9: REPENTANCE (AL-TAWBAH)

9:3 The announcement from God and His Messenger to humanity on the day of the greater pilgrimage to Makkah is that God is free from the ones who are polytheists and so is His Messenger. Then, it will be better for you if you repented. But if you turned away, then, know that you are not ones who frustrate God. Give **you**, (Muhammad), tidings to those who were ungrateful of a painful punishment.

9:6 If anyone of the ones who are polytheists sought asylum with **you**, (Muhammad), then, grant him protection so that he hears the assertions of God. Again, convey **you** him to a place of safety. That is because they are a folk who know not.

9:42 If it had been a near advantage and an easy journey, they would have followed **you**, (Muhammad), except the destination of the journey was distant for them. They will swear by God: If we were able, we would, certainly, have gone forth with you. They will cause themselves to perish. God knows that they are the ones who lie.

9:43 God pardon **you**, (Muhammad)! Why had **you** given permission to them before it becomes clear to **you** those who were sincere and **you** know who are the ones who lie?

9:44 They ask not permission of **you**, (Muhammad), those who believe in God and the Last Day, that they struggle with their wealth and their lives. God is Knowing of the ones who are Godfearing.

9:45 It is only those who ask permission of **you**, (Muhammad), who believe not in God and the Last Day and whose hearts were in doubt, so they go this way and that in their doubts.

9:48 Certainly, they were looking for dissension before. They turned around and around for **you**, (Muhammad), the commands until The Truth drew near, and the command of God became manifest although they were ones who dislike it.

9:50 If lights on **you**, (Muhammad), benevolence, they are raised to anger, but if an affliction lights on **you**, they say: Surely, we took our commands before. They turn away and they are glad.

9:55 So let not their wealth impress **you**, (Muhammad), nor their children. God wants only to punish them in this present life and so that their souls depart while they are ones who are ungrateful.

9:58 Among them there are some who find fault with **you**, (Muhammad), about charities. If they were given a part of it, they were well-pleased, but if they are not given of it, that is when they are displeased.

9:65 If **you**, (Muhammad), had asked them, they would say: Truly, we had only been engaging in idle talk and playing. Say: Was it God and His signs and His Messenger that you had been ridiculing?

9:73 O Prophet! Struggle with the ones who are ungrateful and the ones who are hypocrites and be **you**, (Muhammad), harsh against them. Their place of shelter will be hell. Miserable will be the Homecoming!

9:80 Ask for forgiveness for them or ask not for forgiveness for them, if **you**, (Muhammad), ask for forgiveness for them seventy times, God will never forgive them. That is because they were ungrateful to God and His Messenger. God guides not the folk, the ones who disobey.

9:83 Then, God returned **you**, (Muhammad), to a section of them. They asked **your** permission for going forth. Then, say: You will never ever go forth with me nor fight an enemy with me. You were well-pleased sitting the first time. Then, sit—ones who await with who lagged behind.

9:84 Pray **you** not formally for any of them who died, ever, nor stand up at his grave. Truly, they were ungrateful to God and His Messenger and died while they are ones who disobey.

9:86 When a Chapter of the Quran was caused to descend saying that: Believe in God and struggle along with His Messenger, those imbued with affluence ask permission of **you**, (Muhammad). They said: Forsake us. We would be with the ones who sit at home.

9:92 Nor on those who when they approached **you**, (Muhammad), that **you** would find mounts to carry them, **you** had said: I find not what will carry you. So they turned away while their eyes overflow with tears of grief when they find nothing for them to spend in the way of God.

9:93 The way of blame is only against those who ask **you**, (Muhammad), permission to remain behind and they are rich. They were well-pleased to be with those who stay behind. God set a seal on their hearts so that they know not.

9:101 From around you of the nomads are ones who are hypocrites. From among the people of the city, some grew bold in hypocrisy. **You**, (Muhammad), have not known them but We know them. We will, truly, punish them two times in this world. Again, they will be returned to a tremendous punishment.

9:103 Take charity from their wealth to purify them and make them pure with it. Invoke blessings for them. Truly, **your** entreaties will bring a sense of comfort and rest to them. God is Hearing, Knowing.

9:108 Stand not up in it ever! A place of prostration that was founded from the first day on God-consciousness is more rightful that **you**, (Muhammad), have stood up in it. In it are men who love to cleanse themselves. God loves the ones who cleanse themselves.

9:111-9:112: Truly, God has bought from the ones who believe themselves and their properties, for the Garden is theirs! They fight in the way of God so they kill and are slain. It is a promise rightfully on Him in the Torah and the Gospel and the Quran. Who is more true to His compact than God? Then, rejoice in the good tidings of the bargain that you made in the trade with Him. That, it is the winning the sublime triumph for the repentant worshippers, the ones who praise, the ones who are inclined to fasting, the ones who bow down, the ones who prostrate themselves, the ones who command that which is moral and the ones who prohibit that which is immoral and the ones who guard the ordinances of God. Give **you**, (Muhammad), good tidings to the ones who believe!

114: Chapter 110: The Help (al-Nasr)

110:2-110:3 **You**, (Muhammad), had seen humanity entering into the

way of life of God in units, then, glorify the praise of **your** Lord and ask for
His forgiveness. Truly, He had been ever The Accepter of Repentance.

MADINAH SIGNS IN MAKKAH CHAPTERS

2. CHAPTER 68: THE PEN (AL-QALAM)

68:19 Madinah: Then, a visitation from **your** Lord, (Muhammad), visited
(the garden) while they (the Companions of the Garden) were ones who slept.

> The parable of the Companions of the Garden, 68:17-33: They swore
> an oath that they would pick the fruit from their garden in the morning.
> They made no exception by saying: If God wills (*inshallah*). Then **your**
> Lord, Muhammad, visited their garden while they slept. In the morning
> when they went to their garden, they found the fruit was gone. When they
> saw that there was no fruit to be picked, they said to each other: We have
> certainly gone astray. We are ones who are deprived. The most moderate
> among them said: Did I not ask you why you do not glorify God? The rest
> of them then said: Glory be to God, our Lord! We have been ones who are
> unjust. Then, they began to blame each other and they said: We are heart-
> broken, regretful that we had been defiant. It may be that our Lord will give
> us something better in exchange. We sincerely believe in our Lord. Then
> the Quranic message concludes the parable saying: This is the punishment
> in this world, but the punishment in the world to come if far greater, if only
> they had been knowing.

68:48 Madinah: So be **you**, (Muhammad), patient until the determination of **your** Lord and be not like the Companion of the Great Fish
(Jonah) when he cried out, one who is suppressed by grief.

3. CHAPTER 73: THE ONE WHO IS WRAPPED (AL-MUZZAMMIL)

73:10 Madinah: Have **you**, (Muhammad), patience with regard to what
they say and abandon them with a graceful abandoning.

23. CHAPTER 53: THE STAR (AL-NAJM)

53:32 Madinah: . . .those who avoid the major sins and the indecencies
but the lesser offenses. Truly, **your** Lord is One Who is Extensive in forgiveness. He is greater in knowledge of you when He caused you to grow from
the earth and when you were an unborn child in the wombs of your mothers.
So ascribe not purity to yourselves. He is greater in knowledge of him who
was Godfearing.

50. CHAPTER 17: THE JOURNEY BY NIGHT (AL-ISRA)

17:73 Madinah: And, truly, they were about to persecute **you**, (Muhammad), for what We revealed to **you** so that **you** would devise against Us other
than it. Then, they would take **you** to themselves as a friend.

17:74 Madinah: If We made **you**, (Muhammad), not firm, certainly, **you** were about to incline to them a little.

17:75 Madinah: Then, We would have caused **you**, (Muhammad), to experience a double of this life and a double after dying. Again, **you** would find for **your**self no helper against Us.

17:76 Madinah: They were about to hound **you**, (Muhammad), from the region that they drive **you** out of it. Then, they would not linger in expectation behind **you** but for a little while.

17:77 Madinah: This is, surely, a rule (*sunnah*) with whomever We sent before **you** of Our Messengers. **You** will not find in Our rule (*sunnah*) any revision.

17:79 Madinah: Keep vigil with it in the night as a work of supererogation for **you**, (Muhammad). Perhaps **your** Lord will raise **you** up to a station of one who is praised.

17:80 Madinah: Say: My Lord! Cause **me** to enter a gate in sincerity. Bring **me** out as one who is brought out in sincerity. Assign **me** from that which proceeds from **Your** Presence a helping authority.

51. CHAPTER 10: JONAH (YUNUS)

10:40 Madinah: Of them are some who believe in it and of them are some who believe not in it. **Your** Lord is greater in knowledge of the ones who make corruption.

10:94 Madinah: So if **you**, (Muhammad), had been in uncertainty about what We caused to descend to **you**, then, ask those who recited the Book before **you**. Certainly, The Truth drew near **you** from **your** Lord so **you** have not been among the ones who contest.

10:95 Madinah: **You**, (Muhammad), have not been among those who denied the signs of God, for, then, **you** would be among the ones who are losers.

10:96 Madinah: Truly, those against whom is realized through the Word of **your** Lord, will not believe.

52. CHAPTER 11: HUD (HUD)

11:12 Madinah: So would **you**, (Muhammad), perhaps be one who leaves some of what is revealed to **you**? Or is **your** breast that which is narrowed by it because they say: Why was a treasure not caused to descend to him or an angel drew near him? Truly, **you** are only a warner. God is a Trustee over everything. Or they say: He devised it.

11:17 Madinah: Is he, then, who had been on a clear portent from his Lord, and recounts it from Him as one who bears witness—and before it was the Book of Moses, a leader and a mercy—like them? Those believe in it. Whoever is ungrateful for it among the confederates, he is promised the fire! So be **you**, (Muhammad), not hesitant about it. Truly, it is The Truth from

your Lord, except most of humanity believes not.

53. CHAPTER 12: JOSEPH (YUSUF)

12:3 Madinah: We relate to **you**, (Muhammad), the fairer of narratives
through what We revealed to **you** of this, the Quran, although **you** had been
before this among the ones who are heedless.

55. CHAPTER 6: THE FLOCKS (AL-ANAM)

6:93 Madinah: Who does greater wrong than he who devised lies against
God or said: It was revealed to me, when nothing is revealed to him. Or who
said: I will cause to descend the like of what God caused to descend. If **you**,
(Muhammad), would see when the ones who are unjust are in the perplexity
of death and the angels—the ones who stretch out their hands will say: Re-
linquish your souls. Today, you will be given recompense with the humiliat-
ing punishment for what you had been saying about God other than The
Truth. You had been growing arrogant to His signs.

6:114 Madinah: Will I be looking for an arbiter other than God while it
is He Who caused to descend to you the Book, one that is distinct? Those to
whom We gave the Book, they know that it is one that is sent down by **your**
Lord with The Truth. So **you**, (Muhammad), have not been among the ones
who contest.

57. CHAPTER 31: LUQMAN (LUQMAN)

31:29 Madinah: Have **you**, (Muhammad), not considered that God
causes the nighttime to be interposed into the daytime and causes the daytime
to be interposed into the nighttime and caused the sun to become subservient
and the moon, each run for a term, that which is determined and that God is
Aware of what you do?

58. CHAPTER 34: SHEBA (AL-SABA)

34:6 Madinah: Consider those who were given the knowledge that what
was caused to descend to **you**, (Muhammad), from **your** Lord. It is The Truth
and it guides to a path of The Almighty, The Worthy of Praise.

62. CHAPTER 42: THE CONSULTATION (AL-SHURA)

42:24 Madinah: Or they say: He devised against God a lie. But if God
wills He would have sealed over **your** heart. God blots out falsehood and
verifies The Truth by His Words. Truly, He is Knowing of what is in the
breasts.

66. CHAPTER 46: THE CURVING SANDHILLS (AL-AHQAF)

46:35 Madinah: So have **you**, (Muhammad), patience as endured patiently those imbued with constancy of the Messengers and let them not seek to hasten the Judgment. As, truly, on a Day they will see what they are promised as if they lingered not in expectation but for an hour of daytime. This is delivering the message! Will any be caused to perish but the folk, the ones who disobey?

69. CHAPTER 18: THE CAVE (AL-KAHF)

18:28 Madinah: Have **you**, (Muhammad), patience **your**self with those who call to their Lord in the morning and the evening, wanting His Countenance. Let not **your** eyes pass over them wanting the adornment of this present life. Obey not him whose heart We made neglectful of Our Remembrance and who followed his own desires and whose affair had been excess.

70. CHAPTER 16: THE BEE (AL-NAHL)

16:127 Madinah: Have **you**, (Muhammad), patience and **your** patience is only from God. Feel not remorse over them, nor be **you** troubled about what they plan.

72. CHAPTER 14: ABRAHAM (IBRAHIM)

14:28 Madinah: Have **you**, (Muhammad), not considered those who substituted ingratitude for the divine blessing of God and caused their folk to live in abodes of nothingness?

85. CHAPTER 29: THE SPIDER (AL-ANKABUT)

29:10 Madinah: And of humanity is he who says: We believed in God. But, when he was maligned for the sake of God, he mistook the persecution by humanity for a punishment by God. If help drew near from **your** Lord, they would, surely, say: We had been with you. Is not God greater in knowledge of what is in the breasts of beings?

PART 2. QURANIC COMMANDS ADDRESSED DIRECTLY TO THE PROPHET (2ND PERSON SINGULAR) IN CHRONOLOGICAL ORDER TO "SAY"

MAKKAH CHAPTERS

18. CHAPTER 109: THE UNGRATEFUL (AL-KAFIRUN)
109:1-109:6 <u>Say</u> (Muhammad): O ones who are ungrateful! I worship not what you worship. You are not ones who worship what I worship. I am not one who worships what you worshipped. You are not ones who worship what I worship.

20. CHAPTER 113: THE DAYBREAK (AL-FALAQ)
113:1 <u>Say</u> (Muhammad): I take refuge with the Lord of Daybreak.

21. CHAPTER 114: THE HUMANITY (AL-NAS)
114:1 <u>Say</u> (Muhammad): I take refuge with the Lord of humanity.

22. CHAPTER 112: SINCERE EXPRESSION (AL-IKHLAS)
112:1 <u>Say</u> (Muhammad): He is God, One.

38. CHAPTER 38: SAAD (SAAD)
38:65-38:68 <u>Say</u> (Muhammad): I am only one who warns. There is no god but God, The One, The Omniscient, the Lord of the heavens and the earth and whatever is between them, The Almighty, The Forgiver. <u>Say</u> (Muhammad): It is a serious tiding from which you are ones who turn aside.

39. CHAPTER 7: THE ELEVATED PLACES (AL-ARAF)
7:32 <u>Say</u>: Who forbade the adornment of God that He brought out for His servants. What is the good of His provision? <u>Say</u>: They are for those who believed in this present life and, exclusively, on the Day of Resurrection. Thus, We explain distinctly the signs for a folk who know.

7:33 <u>Say</u> (Muhammad): My Lord forbade not but indecencies—what was manifest or what was inward—and sins and unrightful insolence, to ascribe partners with God when He sends not down for it any authority and that you say about God what you know not.

40. CHAPTER 72: THE JINN (AL-JINN)
72:1 <u>Say</u> (Muhammad): It was revealed to me that a group of jinn listened to me. They said: Truly, we heard a wondrous Recitation.

72:20 <u>Say</u> (Muhammad): Truly, I call only to my Lord. I ascribe not as partners with Him anyone.

72:21 <u>Say</u> (Muhammad): Truly, I possess not the power to hurt nor to bring right mindedness for you.

72:22 <u>Say</u> (Muhammad): Truly, none would grant me protection from God—not anyone! I will never find other than Him that which is a haven

72:25 <u>Say</u> (Muhammad): I am not informed if what you are promised is near, or if my Lord will assign for it a space of time.

42. CHAPTER 25: THE CRITERION (AL-FURQAN)

25:6 <u>Say</u> (Muhammad): It was caused to descend by He who knows the secret in the heavens and the earth. Truly, He had been Forgiving, Compassionate.

25:15 <u>Say</u> (Muhammad): Is that better or the Garden of Infinity that was promised the ones who are Godfearing? It had been a recompense for them and a Homecoming.

25:57 <u>Say</u> (Muhammad): I ask of you no compensation for this but that whoever willed should take himself on a way to his Lord.

25:77 <u>Say</u> (Muhammad): My Lord would not concern Himself with you if it had not been for your supplication, for, surely, you denied so it will be close at hand.

43. CHAPTER 35: THE ORIGINATOR (AL-FATIR)

35:40 <u>Say</u> (Muhammad): Considered you yourselves ascribed associates to whom you call to other than God? Cause me to see what they created in the earth or have they any association in creation of the heavens? Or gave We them a Book so that they have a clear portent from there? Nay! The ones who are unjust promise nothing—some of them to some others—but delusion.

44. CHAPTER 19: MARY (MARYAM)

19:75 <u>Say</u> (Muhammad): Whoever had been in fallacy, The Merciful will prolong his prolonging for him. Until when they would see what they are promised, either the punishment or the Hour, then, they will know whose place is worse and whose army is weak.

45. CHAPTER 20: TA HA (TA HA)

20:105 They will ask **you** about the mountains. <u>Say</u> (Muhammad): My Lord will scatter them a scattering.

20:114 Then, exalted be God, The True King. Hasten not the Recitation before its revelation is decreed to **you**. <u>Say</u> (Muhammad): My Lord! Increase me in knowledge!

20:135 <u>Say</u> (Muhammad): Each is one who is waiting so watch. Then, you will know who are the Companions of the Path without fault and who were truly guided.

46. CHAPTER 56: THE INEVITABLE (AL-WAQIAH)

56:45-56:50 Truly, they had been before that ones who are given ease and they had been persisting in tremendous wickedness. They had been saying: When we died and had been earth dust and bones, will we, then, be ones who are raised up? And our ancient fathers? Say (Muhammad): Truly, the ancient ones and the later ones will be ones who will be gathered to a time appointed on a known Day.

47. CHAPTER 26: THE POETS (AL-SHUARA)

26:216 Then, if they rebelled against you, then, say (Muhammad): Truly, I am free of what you do.

48. CHAPTER 27: THE ANT (AL-NAML)

27:59 Say (Muhammad): The Praise belongs to God. Peace be on His servants, those whom He favored. Is God better or what they ascribe as partner with God?

27:64 Who begins creation, again, will cause it to return and Who provides you from the heaven and the earth. Is there a god besides God? Say (Muhammad): Prepare your proof if you had been ones who are sincere!

27:65 Say (Muhammad): None knows who is in the heavens and the earth, nor the unseen but God. Nor are they aware when they will be raised up.

27:69 Say (Muhammad): Journey through the earth; then, look on how had been the Ultimate End of the ones who sin.

27:72 Say (Muhammad): Perhaps coming close behind you be some of that which you seek to hasten.

27:91-27:93 Truly, I was commanded to worship the Lord of this land which He made sacred and to Whom everything belongs. I was commanded that I be among the ones who submit to God and to recount the Recitation. So whoever was truly guided, then, he is truly guided only for himself. To whoever went astray, say: Truly, I am among the ones who warn. Say (Muhammad): The Praise belongs to God. He will cause you to see His signs and you will recognize them. Your Lord is not One Who is Heedless of what you do.

49. CHAPTER 28: THE STORY (AL-QASAS)

28:49 Say (Muhammad): Then, bring a Book from God that is better guided than these two that I follow it, if you had been ones who are sincere.

28:71 Say (Muhammad): Considered you what if God made the nighttime endless for you until the Day of Resurrection? What god other than God brings you illumination? Will you not, then, hear?

28:72 Say (Muhammad): Considered you what if God made the daytime endless for you until the Day of Resurrection? What god other than God brings you nighttime wherein you rest? Will you not, then, perceive?

50. CHAPTER 17: THE JOURNEY BY NIGHT (AL-ISRA)

17:24 Make yourself low to them (parents), the wing of the sense of humility through mercy. Say (Muhammad): O my Lord! Have mercy on them (parents) even as they raised me when I was small.

17:42 Say (Muhammad): If there had been gods along with Him as they say, then, they would, certainly, be looking for a way to the Possessor of the Throne.

17:48-17:51 Look on how they propounded parables for **you**. So they went astray and they are not able to be on a way. They ask: When we had been bones and broken bits, will we be ones who are raised up in a new creation? Say (Muhammad): Should you be rocks or iron or any creation that is more troublesome in your breasts to raise up. Then, they will say: Who will cause us to return? Say (Muhammad): He Who originated you the first time. Then, they will nod their heads at **you** and say: When will it be? Say (Muhammad): Perhaps it is near.

17:53 Say (Muhammad) to My servants that they should say what is fair. Truly, Satan sows enmity among them. Truly, Satan has been to the human being a clear enemy.

17:56 Say (Muhammad): Call to those whom you claimed other than Him. Then, they are neither in control to remove harm from you nor revise it.

17:81 Say (Muhammad): The Truth drew near and falsehood is vanishing! Truly, falsehood had been made to vanish away.

17:84 Say (Muhammad): Each does according to his same manner. **Your** Lord is greater in knowledge of him who is better guided on the way.

17:85 They will ask **you** about the Spirit. Say (Muhammad): The Spirit is of the command of my Lord. You were not given the knowledge but a little.

17:88 Say (Muhammad): If human kind were gathered together and jinn to bring the like of this Quran, they would not approach the like of it even if some of them had been sustainers of some others. Certainly, We diversified for humanity in this, the Quran, every kind of parable, but most of humanity refused all but disbelief. They would say: We will never believe in **you** until **you** have a fountain gush out of the earth for us.

17:93 Or is there a house of ornament for **you**? Or have **you** ascended up into heaven? We will not believe in **your** ascension until **you** have sent down for us a Book that we recite. Say (Muhammad): Glory be to my Lord! Had I been but a mortal Messenger?

17:95 Say (Muhammad): If there had been angels on earth walking around, ones who are at peace, then, We would certainly have sent down for them from heaven an angel as a Messenger.

17:96 Say (Muhammad): God sufficed as a Witness between me and between you. Truly, He had been of His servants Aware, Seeing.

17:100 <u>Say</u> (Muhammad): If you possessed the treasures of the mercy of my Lord, then, you would hold back for dread of spending. The human being had been ever stingy.

17:107 <u>Say</u> (Muhammad): Believe in it, or believe not. Truly, those who were given the knowledge before it, when it is recounted to them, they fall down on their faces, ones who prostrate.

17:110 <u>Say</u> (Muhammad): Call to God or call to the Merciful. By whatever you call Him, to Him are the Fairer Names. Be **you** not loud in **your** formal prayer nor speak in a low tone and look for a way between.

17:111 <u>Say</u> (Muhammad): The Praise belongs to God Who takes not a son to Himself and there be no associates ascribed with Him in the dominion nor there be for Him need for a protector from humility. Magnify Him a magnification!

51. CHAPTER 10: JONAH (YUNUS)

10:15 When are recounted to them Our signs, clear portents, those who hope not for their meeting with Us said: Bring us a Recitation other than this or substitute it. <u>Say</u> (Muhammad): It be not possible for me to substitute it of my own accord. I follow nothing but what is revealed to me. Truly, I fear if I rebelled against my Lord a punishment on the tremendous Day.

10:16 <u>Say</u> (Muhammad): If God willed, I would not have related it to you nor would He have caused you to recognize it. Surely, I lingered in expectation among you a lifetime before this. Will you not, then, be reasonable?

10:18 They worship other than God things that injure them not, nor profit them. They say: These are our intercessors with God. <u>Say</u> (Muhammad): Are you telling God of what He knows not in the heavens nor in and on the earth? Glory be to Him and exalted is He above partners they ascribe.

10:20 They say: Why was a sign not caused to descend from his Lord? <u>Say</u> (Muhammad): Truly, the unseen belongs only to God. So wait awhile. Truly, I am with you of the ones who are waiting awhile.

10:21 When We caused humanity to experience mercy after tribulation afflicted them, that is when they conspired against Our signs. <u>Say</u> (Muhammad): God is Swifter in planning. Truly, Our messengers write down what you plan.

10:31 <u>Say</u> (Muhammad): Who provides for you from the heaven and the earth? Who controls having the ability to hear and sight? Who brings out the living from the dead and brings out the dead from the living? Who manages the command? They will, then, say: God! <u>Say</u> (Muhammad):Will you not be Godfearing?

10:34 <u>Say</u> (Muhammad): Are there among your ascribed associates with God anyone who begins the creation and, then, causes it to return? <u>Say</u> (Muhammad): God begins the creation. Again, He causes it to return. Then, how you are misled!

10:35 <u>Say</u> (Muhammad): Are there among your ascribed associates with God anyone who guides to The Truth? <u>Say</u> (Muhammad): God guides to The Truth. Has not He who guides to The Truth a better right to be followed than he who guides not unless he himself be guided? What is the matter with you? How you give judgment!

10:38 Or they will say: He devised it. <u>Say</u> (Muhammad): Bring a Chapter of the Quran like it and call to whomever you were able—other than God— if you had been ones who are sincere.

10:41 If they denied **you**, then, **you** <u>say</u> (Muhammad): For me are my actions and for you are your actions. You are free of what I do and I am free of what you do.

10:49 <u>Say</u> (Muhammad): I control not either hurt or profit for myself, but what God willed. To every community there is a term. When their term draws near, neither will they delay it an hour nor will they press it forward.

10:50 <u>Say</u> (Muhammad): Considered you that if His punishment approached you at nighttime or at daytime, for which portion would the ones who sin be ones who seek to hasten?

10:53 They ask **you** to be told: Is it true? <u>Say</u> (Muhammad):Yes! By my Lord it is The Truth and you are not ones who frustrate Him.

10:58 <u>Say</u> (Muhammad): In the grace of God and in His mercy therein let them be glad. That is better than what they gather.

10:59 <u>Say</u> (Muhammad): Considered you from what God caused to descend for you of provision and that you made some of it unlawful and some lawful? <u>Say</u> (Muhammad): Gave God permission to you or devise you against God?

10:69 <u>Say</u> (Muhammad): Truly, those who devise lies against God, they will not prosper.

10:101 <u>Say</u> (Muhammad): Look on what is in the heavens and the earth. Neither the signs nor the warning avail a folk who believe not.

10:102 So wait they awhile but like in the days of those who passed away before them? <u>Say</u> (Muhammad): So wait awhile. I am with you among the ones waiting awhile!

10:104 <u>Say</u> (Muhammad): O humanity! If you were in uncertainty as to my way of life, then, I will not worship those whom you worship other than God. Rather, I worship only God Who will call you to Himself. I was commanded that I be among the ones who believe.

10:108 <u>Say</u> (Muhammad): O humanity! Surely, The Truth drew near you from your Lord so whoever was truly guided, then, he is only truly guided for his own self. Whoever went astray, then, he only goes astray to his own loss. I am not a trustee over you.

52. CHAPTER 11: HUD (HUD)

11:13 <u>Say</u> (Muhammad): Approach you, then, with ten chapters of the

Quran like it, that which is forged, and call to whomever you were able other than God if you had been ones who are sincere.

54. CHAPTER 15: THE ROCKY TRACT (AL-HIJR)
15:89 Say (Muhammad): Truly, I am a clear warner,

55. CHAPTER 6: THE FLOCKS (AL-ANAM)
6:11 Say (Muhammad): Journey through the earth; again, look on how had been the Ultimate End of the ones who deny.

6:12 Say (Muhammad): To whom is whatever is in the heavens and the earth? Say (Muhammad): To God. He prescribed mercy for Himself. He will, certainly, gather you on the Day of Resurrection. There is no doubt in it. Those who lost themselves that Day, then, they will not believe.

6:14 Say (Muhammad): Will I take to myself, other than God, a protector, One Who is Originator of the heavens and the earth? It is He who feeds and He who is never fed. Say (Muhammad): Truly, I was commanded that I be the first who submitted to the One God. **You** have not been among the ones who are polytheists.

6:14 Say (Muhammad): Will I take to myself, other than God, a protector, One Who is Originator of the heavens and the earth? It is He who feeds and He who is never fed. Say (Muhammad): Truly, I was commanded: that I be the first who submitted to the One God. **You** have not been among the ones who are polytheists.

6:15 Say (Muhammad): Truly, I fear if I rebelled against my Lord, the punishment of the tremendous Day!

6:19 Say (Muhammad): Which thing is greater in testimony? Say (Muhammad): God is Witness between me and you. This, the Quran, was revealed to me that I should warn you with it and whomever it reached. Truly, are you bearing witness that there are other gods with God? Say (Muhammad): I bear not such witness. Say (Muhammad): He is not but One God and I am, truly, free from partners you ascribe with Him.

6:37 They said: Why was a sign not sent down to him from his Lord? Say (Muhammad): Truly, God is One Who Has Power over what sign He sends down, except most of them know not.

6:40 Say (Muhammad): Considered you that if the punishment of God approached you or the Hour approached you, would you call to any other than God if you had been ones who are sincere?

6:46 Say (Muhammad): Considered you that if God took your having the ability to hear and your sight and sealed over your hearts, what god other than God restores them to you? Look on how We diversify the signs! Again, they still drew aside.

6:47 Say (Muhammad): Considered you that if the punishment of God approached you suddenly or publicly, will anyone be caused to perish but the folk, the ones who are unjust?

6:50 <u>Say</u> (Muhammad): I say not to you: With me are treasures of God nor that I know the unseen nor say I to you that I am an angel. I follow only what is revealed to me. <u>Say</u> (Muhammad): Are they on the same level— the unwilling to see and the seeing? Will you, then, not reflect?

6:54 When drew near **you**, those who believe in Our signs, <u>say</u> (Muhammad): Peace be to you. Your Lord prescribed mercy for Himself so that anyone of you who did evil in ignorance—again, repented afterwards and made things right—then, truly, He is Forgiving, Compassionate.

6:56 <u>Say</u> (Muhammad): I was prohibited that I worship those whom you call to other than God. <u>Say</u> (Muhammad): I will not follow your desires, for, then, I would have gone astray. I would not be of the ones who are truly guided.

6:57 <u>Say</u> (Muhammad): I am with a clear portent from my Lord and you denied it. I have not of that which you seek to hasten. The determination is with God. He relates The Truth. He is Best of the ones who distinguish truth from falsehood.

6:58 <u>Say</u> (Muhammad): Truly, if with me was what you seek to hasten, the command would be decided between me and between you. God is greater in knowledge of the ones who are unjust.

6:63 <u>Say</u> (Muhammad): Who delivers you from the shadows of the dry land and the sea? You call to Him humbly and inwardly: If **You** were to rescue us from this, we will be of the ones who are thankful.

6:64 <u>Say</u> (Muhammad): God delivers you from them and from every distress. Again, you ascribe partners with Him.

6:65 <u>Say</u> (Muhammad): He is The One Who Has Power to raise up on you a punishment from above you, or from beneath your feet or to confuse you as partisans and to cause you to experience the violence of some of you to one another. Look on how We diversify the signs so that perhaps they will understand!

6:66 **Your** folk denied it and it is The Truth. <u>Say</u> (Muhammad): I am not a trustee over you.

6:71 <u>Say</u> (Muhammad): Will we call to other than God what can neither hurt nor profit us? Are we repelled on our heels after God guided us like one whom the satans lured, bewildered in and on the earth although he has companions who call him to the guidance saying: Approach us? <u>Say</u> (Muhammad): Truly, the guidance of God is The Guidance. We were commanded to submit to the Lord of the worlds.

6:90 Those are those whom God guided. So imitate their guidance. <u>Say</u>: I ask of you no compensation for it. It is not but a reminder for the worlds.

6:109 They swear by God the most earnest sworn oaths that if a sign would draw near them, they would, certainly, believe in it. <u>Say</u> (Muhammad): The signs are only with God. What will cause you to realize that even if the signs were to draw near, they would not believe?

6:135 <u>Say</u> (Muhammad): O my folk! Act according to your ability. Truly, I too am one who acts. Then, you will know for whom the Ultimate End will be the abode. Truly, the ones who are unjust will not prosper.

6:143 Eight diverse pairs; two of sheep and two of goats. <u>Say</u> (Muhammad): Forbade He the two males or the two females? Or what is contained in the wombs of the two females? Tell me with knowledge if you had been ones who are sincere.

6:144 Of the camels two and of cows two, <u>say</u> (Muhammad): Forbade He the two males or the two females or what is contained in the wombs of the two females? Had you been witnesses when God charged you with this? Then, who does greater wrong than he who devised a lie against God to cause humanity to go astray without knowledge. Truly, God guides not the folk, the ones who are unjust.

6:145 <u>Say</u> (Muhammad): I find not in what was revealed to me to taste that which is forbidden to taste, but that it be carrion or blood, that which is shed or the flesh of swine for that, truly, is a disgrace or was hallowed—contrary to moral law—to other than God on it. Then, whoever was driven by necessity other than being one who is willfully disobedient or one who turns away. Then, truly, **your** Lord is Forgiving, Compassionate.

6:147 If they denied **you**, <u>say</u> (Muhammad): Your Lord is the Possessor of Extensive Mercy. His might is not repelled from the folk, ones who sin.

6:148 Those who ascribed partners with God will say: If God willed, neither would we have ascribed partners with God, nor our fathers, nor would we have forbidden anything. Thus, denied those who were before them until they experienced Our might. <u>Say</u> (Muhammad): Is there any knowledge with you that you bring out to us? You follow not but opinion and, then, you only guess.

6:149 <u>Say</u> (Muhammad): God has the conclusive disputation. If He willed, He would have guided you one and all.

6:150 <u>Say</u> (Muhammad). Come on! Bring your witnesses who bear witness that God forbade this. Then, if they bore witness, bear you not witness with them. Follow **you** not the desires of those who denied Our signs and those who believe not in the world to come and they equate others with their Lord.

6:151 <u>Say</u>: Approach now. I will recount what your Lord forbade you Ascribe nothing as partners with Him. Show kindness to the ones who are your parents. Kill not your children from want. We will provide for you and for them. Come not near any indecencies whether these were manifest or what was inward. Kill not a soul which God forbade, unless rightfully. He charged you with that so that perhaps you will be reasonable.

6:158 Look they on only that the angels approach them? Or **your** Lord approach them? Or some signs of **your** Lord approach them? On a Day that approach some signs of **your** Lord, belief will not profit a person if he believed not before, nor earned good because of his belief. Say (Muhammad): Wait awhile! We too are ones who are waiting awhile!

6:161 Say (Muhammad): Truly, my Lord guided me to a straight path, a truth-loving way of life, the creed of Abraham, the monotheist. He had not been of the ones who are polytheists.

6:162 Say (Muhammad): Truly, my formal prayer and my ritual sacrifice and my living and my dying are for God, Lord of all the worlds.

56. CHAPTER 37: THE ONES STANDING IN RANK (AL-SAFFAT)
37:14-37:18 When they saw a sign, they scoff at it. They said: This is not but clear sorcery. Is it when we were dead and had been earth dust and bones that we will, truly, be ones who are raised up and our fathers, the ancient ones? Say (Muhammad): Yes, you will be ones in a state of lowliness.

57. CHAPTER 31: LUQMAN (LUQMAN)
31:25 If **you** had asked them who created the heavens and the earth, they will certainly say: God! Say (Muhammad): The Praise belongs to God! But most of them know not.

58. CHAPTER 34: SHEBA (AL-SABA)
34:3 Those who were ungrateful said: The Hour will not approach us. Say (Muhammad): Yea! By my Lord, it will, certainly, approach you. He is One Who Knows of the unseen. Not an atom's weight escapes from Him in the heavens or in and on the earth, be it smaller than that or greater, but that it had been in a clear Book.

34:22 Say (Muhammad): Call on those whom you claimed other than God. They possess not the weight of an atom in the heavens nor on the earth, nor have they in either any association, nor among them is there any sustainer of Him.

34:24 Say (Muhammad): Who provides for you from the heavens and the earth? Say (Muhammad): God. Truly, are we or you alone on guidance or clearly going astray?

34:25 Say (Muhammad): You will not be asked of what we sinned, nor will we be asked about what you do.

34:26 Say (Muhammad): Our Lord will gather us. Again, He will explain The Truth among us and He is The Opener, The Knowing.

34:27 Say (Muhammad): Cause me to see those whom you caused to join with Him as ascribed associates. No indeed! Nay! He is God, The Almighty, The Wise.

34:30 Say (Muhammad): Yours is the solemn declaration of a Day which you delay not for an hour nor press forward.

34:36 Say (Muhammad): Truly, my Lord extends the provision for whomever He wills and confines it for whom He wills, but most of humanity knows not.

34:39 Say (Muhammad): Truly, my Lord extends the provision for whomever He wills of His servants and confines for him what He wills. Whatever you spent of anything, He will replace it. He is Best of the ones who provide.

34:46 Say (Muhammad): I admonish you in but one thing: That you stand up for God by twos and one by one. Again, reflect. There is not in your companion any madness. He is only a warner to you of a severe punishment in advance of you.

34:47 Say (Muhammad): Whatever compensation I asked of you, that is for you. My compensation is only from God. He is a Witness over everything.

34:48 Say (Muhammad): Truly, my Lord hurls The Truth. He is The Knower of the unseen.

34:49 Say (Muhammad): The Truth drew near and falsehood neither causes to begin nor causes to return.

34:50 Say (Muhammad): If I went astray, truly, I will only go astray with loss for myself. If I was truly guided, it is because of what my Lord reveals to me. Truly, He is Hearing, Ever Near.

59. CHAPTER 39: THE TROOPS (AL-ZUMAR)

39:8 When some distress afflicted the human being, he calls to his Lord as one who turns in repentance to Him. Again, when He granted him divine blessing from Himself, he forgets that for which he had been calling to Him before and he laid on rivals to God to cause others to go astray from His way. Say (Muhammad): Take joy in **your** ingratitude for a while. Truly, you are of the Companions of the Fire.

39:9 Is he one who is morally obligated during the night watch, one who prostrates himself or one who is standing up in prayer being fearful of the world to come and hoping for the mercy of his Lord? Say (Muhammad): Are those who know on the same level as those who know not? Only those imbued with intuition recollect.

39:10 Say (Muhammad): O My servants who believed! Be Godfearing of your Lord. For those who did good in the present, there is benevolence, and the earth of God is One that is Extensive. Only ones who remain steadfast will have their compensation without reckoning.

39:11 Say (Muhammad): Truly, I was commanded to worship God, one who is sincere and devoted in the way of life to Him.

39:13 Say (Muhammad): Truly, I fear if I rebelled against my Lord the punishment of a tremendous Day.

39:14 Say (Muhammad): God alone I worship as one sincere and devoted in the way of life to Him.

39:15 So worship what you would other than Him. Say (Muhammad): Truly, the ones who are losers are those who lost themselves and their people on the Day of Resurrection. Truly, that is a clear loss.

39:38 Truly, if **you** had asked them: Who created the heavens and the earth? They would, certainly, say: God. Say (Muhammad): Considered you what you call to other than God? If God wanted some harm for me, would they (f) (the angels that the ungrateful worship) be ones who remove His harm from me? Or if He wanted mercy for me would they (f) (the angels that the ungrateful worship) be ones who hold back His mercy? Say (Muhammad): God is enough for me. In Him put their trust the ones who put their trust.

39:39 Say (Muhammad): O my folk! Truly, act according to your ability. I am one who acts. You will know

39:43 Or took they to themselves other than God intercessors? Say (Muhammad): Even though they had not been possessing anything and they are not reasonable?

39:44 Say (Muhammad): To God belongs all intercession. His is the dominion of the heavens and the earth. Again, to Him you will be returned.

39:46 Say (Muhammad): O God! One Who is Originator of the heavens and the earth! One Who Knows of the unseen and the visible! **You** will give judgment among **Your** servants about what they had been at variance in it.

39:64 Say (Muhammad): Commanded you me to worship other than God, O ones who are ignorant?

60. CHAPTER 40: THE ONE WHO FORGIVES (AL-GHAFIR)

40:66 Say (Muhammad): Truly, I was prohibited from worshipping those whom you call to other than God, because the clear portents drew near me from my Lord. I was commanded to submit to the Lord of the worlds.

61. CHAPTER 41: THEY WERE EXPLAINED DISTINCTLY (AL-FUSSILAT)

41:6 Say (Muhammad): I am only a mortal like you. It is revealed to me that your God is God, One; so go straight to Him and ask for forgiveness from Him, and woe to the ones who are polytheists—those who give not the purifying alms.

41:9 Say (Muhammad): Truly, are you ungrateful to Him Who created the earth in two days? Assign you to Him rivals? That is the Lord of the worlds!

41:13 But if they turned aside, then, say: I warned you of a thunderbolt like the thunderbolt of Aad and Thamud.

41:44 If We made this a non-Arabic Recitation, they would have said: Why were His signs not explained distinctly: A non-Arab tongue and an Arab! Say (Muhammad): It is a guidance for those who believe and a healing.

As for those who believed not, there is a heaviness in their ears and blindness in their hearts. Those are given notice from a far place.

41:52 Say (Muhammad): Considered you that even though it had been from God, again, you were ungrateful for it. Who is one who goes more astray than he who is in wide breach?

62. CHAPTER 42: THE CONSULTATION (AL-SHURA)

42:15 Then, for that, call to this. Go **you** straight as **you** were commanded. Follow not their desires. Say (Muhammad): I believed in what God caused to descend from a Book. I was commanded to be just among you. God is our Lord and your Lord. For us are our actions and for you, your actions. There is no disputation between us and between you. God will gather us together. To Him is the Homecoming.

63. CHAPTER 43: THE ORNAMENTS (AL-ZUKHRUF)

43:80-43:90 Assume they (the ungrateful) that We hear not their secret thoughts and their conspiring secretly? Yea! Our messengers are near them writing down. Say (Muhammad): If The Merciful had had a son, then, I would be first of the ones who worship. Glory be to the Lord of the heavens and the earth, the Lord of the Throne, from all that they allege! So let them engage in idle talk and play until they encounter their Day which they are promised. It is He Who is in the heaven, God, and on the earth, God. And He is The Wise, The Knowing. Blessed be He to whom belongs the dominion of the heavens and the earth and whatever is between them and with Whom is the knowledge of the Hour and to Whom you will be returned. Those whom they call to possess no power other than Him for intercession, only whoever bore witness to The Truth, and they know. If **you** had asked them: Who created them? They would, certainly, say: God. Then, how are they misled? His saying: O my Lord! Truly, these are a folk who believe not, overlook them and say: Peace. They will know.

65. CHAPTER 45: THE ONES WHO KNEEL (AL-JATHIYAH)

45:26 Say (Muhammad): God gives you life. Again, He causes you to die. Again, He will gather you on the Day of Resurrection in which there is no doubt but most of humanity knows not.

66. CHAPTER 46: THE CURVING SANDHILLS (AL-AHQAF)

46:4 Say (Muhammad): Considered you what you call to other than God? Cause me to see what of the earth they created. Have they an association in the heavens? Bring me a Book from before this, or a vestige of knowledge if you had been ones who are sincere.

46:8 Or they say: He devised it. Say (Muhammad): If I devised it, you still possess nothing for me against God. He is greater in knowledge of what you press on about. He sufficed as a Witness between me and between you. He is The Forgiving, The Compassionate.

46:9 <u>Say</u> (Muhammad): I had not been an innovation among the Messengers, nor am I informed of what will be inflicted on me, nor with you. I follow only what is revealed to me and I am only a clear warner.

69. CHAPTER 18: THE CAVE (AL-KAHF)

18:22-18:24 They will say: They were three, the fourth of them being their dog. They will say: They were five, the sixth of them being their dog, guessing at the unseen. They will say: They were seven, the eighth of them being their dog. <u>Say</u> (Muhammad): My Lord is greater in knowledge of their amount. No one knows them but a few, so argue not about them but with a manifest argumentation and ask not for advice about them of anyone of them. Surely, he will not say about something: Truly, I will be one who does that tomorrow, but that you add: If God wills. Remember **your** Lord when **you** had forgotten. <u>Say</u> (Muhammad): Perhaps my Lord will guide me nearer to right mindedness than this.

18:26 <u>Say</u> (Muhammad): God is greater in knowledge of how long they lingered in expectation. To Him belongs the unseen of the heavens and the earth. How well He perceives and how well He hears! Other than him, they have no protector and He ascribes no one partners in His determination.

18:29 <u>Say</u> (Muhammad): The Truth is from your Lord. Then, let whoever willed, believe, and let whoever willed, disbelieve. Truly, We made ready a fire for the ones who are unjust. They will be enclosed by its large tent. If they cry for help, they will be helped with rain, water like molten copper that will scald their faces. Miserable was the drink and how evil a place of rest!

18:103 <u>Say</u> (Muhammad): Shall We tell you who will be ones who are losers by their actions?

18:109 <u>Say</u> (Muhammad): If the sea had been ink for the Words of my Lord, the sea would come to an end before the Words of my Lord came to an end even if We brought about replenishment the like of it.

18:110 <u>Say</u> (Muhammad): I am only a mortal like you. It is revealed to me that your God is One, so whoever had been hoping for the meeting with his Lord, let him do with his actions as one in accord with morality and ascribe no partners—in the worship of his Lord, ever.

70. CHAPTER 16: THE BEE (AL-NAHL)

16:102 <u>Say</u> (Muhammad):The hallowed Spirit sent it down from **your** Lord with The Truth to make firm those who believed and as a guidance and good tidings to the ones who submit to God.

72. CHAPTER 14: ABRAHAM (IBRAHIM)

14:30 They made rivals with God, causing others to go astray from His way. Say (Muhammad): Take joy, but, truly, your homecoming is the fire!

14:31 Say (Muhammad) to My servants who have believed that they should perform the formal prayers and spend from what We have provided them secretly and in public before a Day approaches in which there is neither trading nor befriending.

73. CHAPTER 21: THE PROPHETS (AL-ANBIYA)

21:24 Or took they gods to themselves other than He? Say (Muhammad): Prepare your proof. This is a Remembrance for him who is with me and a Remembrance of him before me. Nay! Most of them know not The Truth, so they are ones who turn aside.

21:42 Say (Muhammad): Who will guard you in the nighttime and the daytime from The Merciful? Nay! They, from the Remembrance of their Lord, are ones who turn aside.

21:45 Say (Muhammad): I warn you only by the revelation. But hear not the unwilling to hear, the calling to them when they are warned.

21:108 Say (Muhammad): It is only revealed to me that your god is One God. Will you, then, be ones who submit to God?

21:109 But if they turned away, then, say (Muhammad): I proclaimed to you all equally. I am not informed whether what you are promised is near or far.

74. CHAPTER 23: THE BELIEVERS (AL-MUMINUN)

23:84 Say (Muhammad): To whom belongs the earth and whoever is in it if you had been knowing?

23:85 They will say: To God! Say (Muhammad): Will you then not recollect?

23:86 Say (Muhammad): Who is the Lord of the seven heavens and Lord of the Sublime Throne?

23:87 They will say: It belongs to God! Say (Muhammad): Then, will you not be Godfearing?

23:88 Say (Muhammad): In whose hand is the kingdom of everything and He grants protection? No one is granted protection against Him if you had been knowing.

23:89 They will say: It belongs to God! Say (Muhammad): How, then, are you under a spell!

23:93-23:97 Say (Muhammad): My Lord! If You will cause me to see what they are promised, then, assign me not, my Lord, to the folk, the ones who are unjust. Truly, We cause **you** to see what We promise them as certainly ones who have power. Drive **you** back evil deeds with what is fairer. We are greater in knowledge of what they allege. Say (Muhammad): My Lord! I take refuge with **You** from the evil suggestions of the satans.

23:118 Say (Muhammad): My Lord! Forgive and have mercy. **You** are Best of the ones who are most merciful.

75. CHAPTER 32: THE PROSTRATION (AL-SAJDAH)

32:11 <u>Say</u> (Muhammad):The angel of death who was charged with you, will call you to itself. Again, you will be returned to your Lord.

32:29 <u>Say</u> (Muhammad): On the Day of Victory there will be no profit for those who disbelieved if they, then, have belief nor will they be given respite.

76. CHAPTER 52: THE MOUNT (AL-TUR)

52:31 <u>Say</u> (Muhammad): Await for I am with the ones who are waiting.

77. CHAPTER 67: THE DOMINION (AL-MULK)

67:23 <u>Say</u> (Muhammad): It is He who caused you to grow and assigned you the ability to hear, sight, and minds. But you give little thanks!

67:24 <u>Say</u> (Muhammad): It is He who made you numerous on the earth and to Him you will be assembled.

67:26 <u>Say</u> (Muhammad): The knowledge of this is only with God and I am only a clear warner.

67:28 <u>Say</u> (Muhammad): Considered you if God would cause me to perish and whoever is with me or had mercy on us, who will grant protection to the ones who are ungrateful from a painful punishment?

67:29 <u>Say</u> (Muhammad): He is The Merciful. We believed in Him and in Him we put our trust. Then, you will know who he is, one who is clearly gone astray.

67:30 <u>Say</u> (Muhammad): Considered you? If it came to be in the morning that your water be sinking into the ground, who approaches you with assistance from water springs?

84. CHAPTER 30: THE ROMANS (AL-RUM)

30:42 <u>Say</u> (Muhammad): Journey through the earth. Then, look on how had been the Ultimate End of those who were before. Most of them had been ones who are polytheists.

85. CHAPTER 29: THE SPIDER (AL-ANKABUT)

29:20 <u>Say</u> (Muhammad): Journey through the earth. Then, look on how He began the creation. Again, God will cause the last growth to grow. Truly, God is Powerful over everything.

29:50 They said: Why were signs not caused to descend to him from his Lord? <u>Say</u> (Muhammad): The signs are only with God. I am only a warner, one who makes clear.

29:52 <u>Say</u> (Muhammad): God sufficed as a witness between me and between you. He knows whatever is in the heavens and the earth. Those who believed in falsehood and were ungrateful to God, those, they are the ones who are losers.

29:63 If **you** had asked them: Who sent down water from heaven and gave life by it to the earth after its death, certainly, they would say: God! <u>Say</u> (Muhammad): The Praise belongs to God! Nay! Most of them are not reasonable.

MADINAH CHAPTERS

87. CHAPTER 2: THE COW (AL-BAQARAH)

2:80 They said: The fire will never touch us, but for numbered days. <u>Say</u>: Took you to yourselves a compact from God? If so, God never breaks His compact; or say you about God what you know not?

2:91 When it was said to them: Believe in what God caused to descend, they said: We believe in what was caused to descend to us. They are ungrateful for what is beyond it, while it is The Truth, that which establishes as true what is with them. <u>Say</u>: Why, then, kill you the Prophets of God before if you had been ones who believe?

2:97 <u>Say</u> (Muhammad): Whoever had been an enemy of Gabriel knows, then, truly, it was sent down through him to **your** heart with the permission of God, that which establishes as true what was before it, and as a guidance and good tidings for the ones who believe.

2:111 They said: None will enter the Garden, but ones who had been Jews or Christians. That is their own fantasies. <u>Say</u> (Muhammad): Prepare your proof if you had been ones who are sincere.

2:120 The Jews will never be well-pleased with **you**, nor the Christians until **you** have followed their creed. <u>Say</u> (Muhammad): Truly, guidance of God. It is the guidance. If **you** had followed their desires after what drew near **you** of the knowledge, there is not for **you** from God either a protector or a helper.

2:135 They said: Be you ones who are Jews or Christians, you would be truly guided. <u>Say</u> (Muhammad): Nay! We follow the creed of Abraham, a monotheist, and he had not been of the ones who are polytheists.

2:139 <u>Say</u> (Muhammad): Argue you with us about God? He is our Lord and your Lord. To us are our actions, and to you are your actions. We are to Him ones who are sincere and devoted.

2:140 Or say you about Abraham and Ishmael and Isaac and Jacob and the Tribes had been ones who became Jews or were Christians? <u>Say</u>: Are you greater in knowledge or God? Who does greater wrong than he who had been keeping back testimony from God that is with him, and God is not One Who is Heedless of what you do.

2:142 The fools among humanity say: What turned them from their direction of formal prayer to which they had been towards? <u>Say</u> (Muhammad): To God belongs the East and the West. He guides whom He wills to a straight path.

2:189 They ask **you** about the new moons. <u>Say</u> (Muhammad): They are appointed times for humanity, and the pilgrimage to Makkah. It is not virtuous conduct that you approach houses from the back. Rather, virtuous conduct was to be Godfearing, and approach houses from their front doors. Be Godfearing of God so that perhaps you will prosper.

2:215 They ask **you** what they should spend. <u>Say</u> (Muhammad): Whatever you spent for good is for the ones who are your parents and the nearest kin and the orphans and the needy and the traveler of the way. Whatever good you accomplish, then, truly, God is Knowing of it.

2:217 They ask **you** about the Sacred Month and fighting in it. <u>Say</u> (Muhammad): Fighting in it is deplorable and barring from the way of God and ingratitude to Him. To bar from the Masjid al-Haram and expelling people from it are more deplorable with God. Persecution is more deplorable than killing. They cease not to fight you until they repel you from your way of life, if they are able. Whoever of you goes back on his way of life, then, dies while he is one who is ungrateful, those, their actions were fruitless in the present and in the world to come. Those will be the Companions of the Fire. They are ones who will dwell in it forever.

2:219-2:220 They ask **you** about intoxicants and gambling. <u>Say</u> (Muhammad): In both of them there is deplorable sin and profits for humanity. Their sin is more deplorable than what is profitable. They ask **you** how much they should spend. <u>Say</u> (Muhammad): The extra. Thus, God makes manifest His signs to you so that perhaps you will reflect on the present and the world to come. They ask **you** about orphans. <u>Say</u> (Muhammad): Making things right for them is better. And if you intermix with them, then they are your brothers/sisters. God knows the one who makes corruption from the one who makes things right. If God willed, He would have overburdened you. Truly, God is Almighty, Wise.

2:222 They ask **you** about menstruation. <u>Say</u> (Muhammad): It is an impurity, so withdraw from your wives during menstruation. Come not near them (f) until they cleanse themselves. Then, when they (f) cleansed themselves, approach them (f) as God commanded you. Truly, God loves the contrite and He loves the ones who cleanse themselves.

88. CHAPTER 8: THE SPOILS OF WAR (AL-ANFAL)

8:1 They ask **you** about the spoils of war. <u>Say</u> (Muhammad): The spoils of war belong to God and the Messenger so be Godfearing of God and make things right among you. Obey God and his Messenger if you had been ones who believe.

8:38 <u>Say</u> (Muhammad) to those who ere ungrateful: If they refrain themselves, what is past will be forgiven. If they repeat after that, the customs that have passed away of the ancient ones are a warning.

8:70 O Prophet! <u>Say</u> (Muhammad): to those who are in your hands of the prisoners of war: If God knows any good in your hearts, He will give you better than that that was taken from you and He will forgive you, and God is Forgiving, Compassionate.

89. CHAPTER 3: THE FAMILY OF IMRAN (AL-I IMRAN)

3:12 Say (Muhammad) to those who are ungrateful: You will be vanquished and are to be assembled into hell. It is a miserable Final Place.

3:15 Say (Muhammad): Shall I tell you of better than that? For those who were Godfearing, with their Lord are Gardens beneath which rivers run. They are ones who will dwell in them forever with purified spouses and contentment from God. God is Seeing His servants,

3:20 So if they argued with **you**, then say: I submitted my face to God as have those who followed me. Say (Muhammad) to those who were given the Book and to the unlettered: Have you submitted to God? If they submitted to God, then, surely, they were truly guided. If they turned away, then, on **you** is only delivering the message. God is Seeing of His servants.

3:26 Say (Muhammad): O God! The One Who is Sovereign of Dominion, **You** have given dominion to whom **You** have willed, and **You** have torn away dominion from whom **You** have willed. **You** have rendered powerful whom **You** have willed, and **You** have abased whom **You** have willed. In **Your** hand is the good. Truly, **You** are Powerful over everything.

3:29 Say (Muhammad): Whether you conceal what is in your breasts or show it, God knows it and He knows whatever is in the heavens and whatever is in and on the earth. God is Powerful over everything.

3:31 Say (Muhammad): If you had been loving God, then, follow me. God will love you and forgive you your impieties. God is Forgiving, Compassionate.

3:32 Say (Muhammad): Obey God and the Messenger. Then, if they turned away, then, truly, God loves not the ones who are ungrateful.

3:61 Then, to whoever argued with **you** about it after what drew near **you** of the knowledge, say (Muhammad): Approach now! Let us call to our children and your children and our women and your women and ourselves and yourselves. Again we will humbly supplicate, and we lay the curse of God on the ones who lie.

3:64 Say: O People of the Book! Approach now to a word common between us and between you that we worship none but God and ascribe nothing as partners with Him, that none of us take others to ourselves as lords besides God. If they turned away, then, say: Bear witness that we are ones who submit to God.

3:84 Say (Muhammad): We believed in God and what was caused to descend to us and what was caused to descend to Abraham and Ishmael and Isaac and Jacob and the Tribes and what was given to Moses and Jesus and the Prophets from their Lord. We separate and divide not between anyone of them and we are ones who submit to Him.

3:93 All food had been allowed to the Children of Jacob, but what Jacob, (Israel), forbade to himself before the Torah is sent down. Say: Then, approach with the Torah and recount it if you had been ones who are sincere.

3:95 Say: God was Sincere, so follow the creed of Abraham—a monotheist—and he had not been among the ones who are polytheists.

3:98 Say (Muhammad): O People of the Book! Why be ungrateful for the signs of God? God is Witness over what you do.

3:99 Say (Muhammad): O People of the Book! Why bar you from the way of God he who believed, desiring crookedness when you are witnesses? God is not One Who is Heedless of what you do.

3:119 Lo, behold! You are those imbued with love for them, but they love you not. You believed in the Book, all of it. When they met you, they said: We believe. But when they went privately, they bit the tips of their fingers at you in rage. Say (Muhammad): Die in your rage. Truly God is Knowing of what is within the breasts.

3:154 Again, He caused to descend safety for you after lament. Sleepiness overcomes a section of you while a section caused themselves grief thinking of God without right, a thought out of the Age of Ignorance. They say: Have we any part in the command? Say (Muhammad): Truly, the command is entirely from God. They conceal within themselves what they show not to **you**. They say: If there had been for us any part in the command, we would not be killed here. Say (Muhammad): Even if you had been in your houses, those would have departed—whom it was prescribed they be slain—for the Final Place of sleeping, so that God tests what is in your breasts and He proves what is in your hearts. God is Knowing of what is in the breasts.

3:165 Why, when an affliction lit on you, surely, you lit two times its like on them. Say (Muhammad):Where is this from? Say (Muhammad): It is from yourselves. Truly, God is Powerful over everything.

3:168 Those who said to their brothers while they sat back: If they obeyed us, they would not have been slain. Say (Muhammad): Then, drive off death from yourselves, if you had been ones who are sincere.

3:183 To those who said: Truly, God made a compact with us that we believe not in a Messenger until He approaches with a sacrifice to be consumed by the fire, say (Muhammad): Surely, Messengers brought about to you before me the clear portents and even of what you spoke. Then, why have you killed them if you had been ones who are sincere?

90. CHAPTER 33: THE CONFEDERATES (AL-AHZAB)

33:16 Say (Muhammad): Running away will never profit you that you ran away from death or killing, then, you will be given enjoyment but for a little.

33:17 Say (Muhammad): Who will save you from harm from God if He wanted evil for you or wanted mercy for you? They will not find for themselves other than God a protector or a helper.

33:28 O Prophet! <u>Say</u> (Muhammad) to **your** spouses: If you had been wanting this present life and its adornment, then, approach now. I will give you enjoyment and set you (f) free, releasing gracefully.

33:63 Humanity asks **you** about the Hour. <u>Say</u> (Muhammad): The knowledge of it is only with God. What will cause **you** to recognize that perhaps the Hour be near?

92. CHAPTER 4: THE WOMEN (AL-NISA)

4:77 Have **you** not considered those who when it was said to them: Limit your hands from warfare and perform the formal prayer and give the purifying alms? Then, when fighting was prescribed for them, there was a group of people among them who dread humanity, even dreading God or with a more severe dreading, and they said: Our Lord! Why had **You** prescribed fighting for us? Why had **You** not postponed it for another near term for us? <u>Say</u> (Muhammad): The enjoyment of the present is little and the world to come is better. For whomever was Godfearing, you will not be wronged in the least.

4:78 Wherever you be, death will overtake you, even if you had been in imposing towers. When benevolence lights on them, they say: This is from God. When an evil deed lights on them, they say: This is from **you**. <u>Say</u> (Muhammad): All is from God. So what is with these folk that they understand almost no discourse?

4:127 They ask you for advice about women. <u>Say</u> (Muhammad): God pronounces to you about them (f) and what is recounted to you in the Book about women who have orphans, those to whom (f) you give not what was prescribed for them (f) because you prefer that you marry them (f) and about the ones taken advantage of due to weakness among children and that you stand up for the orphans with equity. Whatever you accomplish of good, then, truly, God had been Knowing of it.

4:176 They ask **you** for advice. <u>Say</u> (Muhammad): God pronounces to you about indirect heirs. If a man perished and he be without children and he has a sister, then, for her is half of what he left. He inherits from her if she be without children. If there had been two sisters, then, for them (f), two-thirds of what he left. If there had been brothers/sisters, men and women, the man will have the like allotment as two females. God makes manifest to you so that you go not astray. God is Knowing of everything.

96. CHAPTER 13: THUNDER (AL-RAD)

13:16 <u>Say</u> (Muhammad): Who is the Lord of the heavens and the earth? <u>Say</u> (Muhammad): God! <u>Say</u> (Muhammad): Took you to yourselves other than Him protectors? They control not themselves, neither profiting nor hurting. <u>Say</u> (Muhammad): Are the unwilling to see on the same level as the seeing? Are the shadows on the same level as the light? Made they ascribed associates with God who created as His creation so that creation resembled one another to them? Say (Muhammad): God is One Who is Creator of everything. He is The One, The Omniscient.

13:27 Those who were ungrateful say: Why was a sign not caused to descend to him from his Lord? Say (Muhammad): Truly, God causes to go astray whom He wills and guides to Himself whomever was penitent,

13:30 Thus, We sent **you** to a community. Surely, passed away other communities before it so that **you** would recount to them what We revealed to **you** and they are ungrateful to The Merciful. Say (Muhammad): He is my Lord. There is no god but He. In Him I put my trust and to Him I am turning in repentance.

13:33 Is He, then, One Who Sustains Every Soul for what it earned? Yet they ascribe associates with God! Say (Muhammad): Name them! Or will you tell Him of what He knows not in the earth? Or name you only them in the manifest sayings? Nay! Made to appear pleasing to those who were ungrateful was their planning and they were barred from the way. Whomever God causes to go astray, for him there is no one who guides.

13:36 Those to whom We gave the Book are glad at what was caused to descend to **you**. There are among the confederates some who reject some of it. Say (Muhammad): I was commanded to worship only God and not to ascribe partners with Him. I call to Him and to Him is my destination.

13:43 Those who were ungrateful say: **You** are not one who is sent. Say (Muhammad): God sufficed as a witness between me and between you and whoever has knowledge of the Book.

102. CHAPTER 24: THE LIGHT (AL-NUR)

24:30 Say (Muhammad) to the males, ones who believe, to lower their sight and keep their private parts safe. That is purer for them. Truly, God is Aware of what they craft.

24:31 Say (Muhammad) to the females, ones who believe, to lower their (f) sight and keep their (f) private parts safe and show not their (f) adornment but what is manifest of it. Let them (f) draw their head coverings over their (f) bosoms; and not show their (f) adornment but to their (f) husbands or their (f) fathers or the fathers of their (f) husbands or their sons or the sons of their (f) husbands or their (f) brothers or the sons of their (f) brothers or the sons of their (f) sisters or their (f) women, or what their (f) right hands possessed, or the ones who heed, imbued with no sexual desire among the men or small male children to whom was not manifest nakedness of women. Let them (f) not stomp their feet so as to be known what they (f) conceal of their adornment. Turn to God altogether for forgiveness. O the ones who believe, so that perhaps you will prosper.

24:53 They swore by God their most earnest oaths that if **you** would command them, they would go forth. Say (Muhammad): Swear not; honorable obedience is better. Truly, God is Aware of what you do.

24:54 <u>Say</u> (Muhammad): Obey God and obey the Messenger. But if you turn away, then, on him was only what was loaded on him, and on you was only what was loaded on you. If you obey him, you will be truly guided. There is not a duty on the Messenger but the delivering of the clear message.

103. CHAPTER 22: THE PILGRIMAGE (AL-HAJJ)

22:49 <u>Say</u> (Muhammad): O humanity! Truly, I am only a clear warner to you.

22:68 If they disputed with **you**, then, **you** <u>say</u> (Muhammad): God is greater in knowledge about what you do.

22:72 When Our signs are recounted to them, clear portents, **you** will recognize on the faces of those who were ungrateful, that they are the ones who are rejected. They are about to rush upon those who recount Our signs to them. <u>Say</u> (Muhammad): Shall I tell you of worse than that? God promised the fire to those who were ungrateful. Miserable will be the Homecoming!

106. CHAPTER 49: THE INNER APARTMENTS (AL-HUJURAT)

49:14 The nomads said: We believed. <u>Say</u> (Muhammad) to them: You believe not. But say: We submitted to God, for belief enters not yet into your hearts. But if you obey God and His Messenger, He will not withhold your actions at all. Truly, God is Forgiving, Compassionate.

49:16 <u>Say</u> (Muhammad): Would you teach God about your way of life while God knows whatever is in the heavens and whatever is in and on the earth? God is Knowing of everything.

49:17 They show grace to **you** that they submitted to God. <u>Say</u> (Muhammad): Show you submission to God as grace to me? Nay! God shows grace to you in that He guided you to belief if you, truly, had been ones who are sincere.

108. CHAPTER 64: THE MUTUAL LOSS AND GAIN (AL-TAGHABUN)

64:7 Those who were ungrateful claimed that they will never be raised up. <u>Say</u> (Muhammad): Yea! By my Lord, you will, certainly, be raised up. Again, you will be told of what you did. That is easy for God.

110. CHAPTER 62: THE CONGREGATION (AL-JUMUAH)

62:6 <u>Say</u> (Muhammad): O those who became Jews! If you claimed that you are the protectors of God to the exclusion of humanity, then, covet death if you had been ones who are sincere.

62:8 <u>Say</u> (Muhammad): Truly, the death that you run away from, then, it will be, truly, that which you encounter. Again, you will be returned to the One Who Knows of the unseen and the visible and He will tell you what you had been doing.

62:11 When they considered a transaction or a diversion, they broke away toward it, and left **you** as one who is standing up. <u>Say</u> (Muhammad): What is with God is better than any diversion or than any transaction. God is Best of the ones who provide.

111. Chapter 48: The Victory (al-Fath)
48:11 The ones who were left behind will say among the nomads: Our property and our people occupied us, so ask forgiveness for us. They say with their tongues what is not in their hearts. <u>Say</u> (Muhammad): Who then has sway over you against God at all if He has wanted to harm you or has wanted to bring you profit? Nay! God has been Aware of what you do.

48:15 The ones who are left behind will say when you set out to take the gains: Let us follow you. They want to substitute for the assertion of God. <u>Say</u> (Muhammad): You will not follow us. Thus, God said before; then, they will say: Nay! You are jealous of us. Nay! They had not been understanding, but a little.

112. Chapter 5: The Table Spread with Food (al-Maida)
5:4 They ask **you** what was permitted to them. <u>Say</u> (Muhammad): That which is good was permitted to you and what you taught of hunting creatures, as one who teaches hunting dogs of what God taught you. So eat of what they seized for you and remember the Name of God over it and be Godfearing of God. Truly, God is Swift in reckoning.

5:17 Certainly, ungrateful were those who said: Truly, God is the Messiah, the son of Mary. <u>Say</u> (Muhammad): Who, then, has any sway over God? If He wanted to He would cause the Messiah son of Mary and his mother to perish and whatever is in and on the earth altogether. To God belongs the dominion of the heavens and the earth and what is between the two. He creates what He wills. God is Powerful over everything.

5:18 The Jews and Christians said: We are the children of God and His beloved. <u>Say</u> (Muhammad):Why, then, does He punish you for your impieties? Nay! You are mortals whom He created. He forgives whom He wills and He punishes whom He wills. To God belongs the dominion of the heavens and the earth and what is even between the two. To Him is the Homecoming!

5:59 <u>Say</u> (Muhammad): O People of the Book! Seek you revenge on us because we believed in God and what was caused to descend to us and what was caused to descend before, while, truly, most of you are ones who disobey?

5:60 <u>Say</u> (Muhammad): Will I tell **you** of worse than that as a reward from God? He whom God cursed and with whom He was angry and He made some of them into apes and swine who worshiped the false deities. Those are worse placed and ones who go astray from the right way.

5:68 <u>Say</u> (Muhammad): O People of the Book! You are not based on anything until you adhere to the Torah and the Gospel and what was caused to descend to you from your Lord. Certainly, many of them increase by what was caused to descend to **you** from **your** Lord in defiance and ingratitude. So grieve not for folk, the ones who are ungrateful.

5:76 <u>Say</u>: Worship you other than God what controls neither hurt nor profit for you? And God, He is The Hearing, The Knowing.

5:77 <u>Say</u>: O People of the Book! Go not beyond limits in your way of life but with The Truth and follow not the desires of the folk who, surely, went astray before. And they caused many to go astray. They themselves went astray from the right way.

5:100 <u>Say</u> (Muhammad): Not on the same level are the bad and what is good even if the prevalence of the bad impressed you. So be Godfearing of God, O those imbued with intuition, so that perhaps you will prosper.

113. CHAPTER 9: REPENTANCE (AL-TAWBAH)

9:24 <u>Say</u> (Muhammad): If had been your fathers and your children and your brothers/sisters and your spouses and your kinspeople and the wealth you gained and the transactions you dread slacken and the dwellings with which you are well-pleased were more beloved to you than God and His Messenger and struggling in His Way, then, await until God brings His command. God guides not the folk, ones who disobey.

9:51 <u>Say</u> (Muhammad): Nothing will light on us but what God had been prescribing for us. He is our Defender. In God let the ones who believe put their trust.

9:52 <u>Say</u> (Muhammad): Are you watching for something, but one of the two fairer things to befall us? We watch for you, whether God will light on you a punishment from Him or from our hands. So watch! We are ones who are waiting with you.

9:53 <u>Say</u> (Muhammad): Spend willingly or unwillingly. There will be only non-acceptance. Truly, you, you had been a folk, ones who disobey.

9:61 Among them are those who malign the Prophet and say: He is unquestioning. <u>Say</u> (Muhammad):He is unquestioning of what is good for you. He believes in God and believes in ones who believe. He is a mercy to those of you who believed. Those of you who malign the Messenger of God, for them is a painful punishment.

9:64 The ones who are hypocrites are fearful that should be sent down against them a Chapter of the Quran to tell them what is in their hearts. <u>Say</u> (Muhammad): Ridicule us, but, truly, God is One Who Drives Out that of which you are fearful.

9:65 If **you** had asked them, they would say: Truly, we had only been engaging in idle talk and playing. <u>Say</u> (Muhammad):Was it God and His signs and His Messenger that you had been ridiculing?

9:81 The ones who are left behind were glad of their positions behind the Messenger of God. They disliked struggling with their wealth and themselves in the way of God. They said: Move not forward in the heat. Say (Muhammad): The fire of hell has more severe heat. Would that they had been understanding!

9:83 Then, God returned **you** to a section of them. They asked **your** permission for going forth. Say (Muhammad): You will never ever go forth with me nor fight an enemy with me. You were well-pleased sitting the first time. Then, sit—ones who await with who lagged behind.

9:94 They will make excuses to you when you returned to them. Say (Muhammad): Make no excuses. We will never believe you. Surely, God told us news about you. God and His Messenger will consider your actions. Again, you will be returned to One Who Knows the unseen and the visible. Then, He will tell you of what you had been doing.

9:105 Say (Muhammad): Act! God will consider your actions and so will His Messenger and the ones who believe. You will be returned to Him, One Who Knows of the unseen and the visible. Then, He will tell you what you had been doing.

9:129 But if they turned away, say: God is enough for me. There is no god but He. In Him I put my trust. He is the Lord of the Sublime Throne.

Part 3. Other Quranic Commands Addressed Directly to the Prophet (2nd person singular) in Chronological Order

Makkah Chapters

1. Chapter 96: The Blood Clot (al-Alaq)
96:1 <u>Recite</u> in the Name of **your** Lord Who created.

96:3 <u>Recite</u>: **Your** Lord is the Most Generous,

96:19 No indeed! Truly, <u>obey</u> **you** him not but <u>prostrate</u> **your**self to God and be near to Him.

2. Chapter 68: The Pen (al-Qalam)
68:40 <u>Ask</u> them, (Muhammad), then, which of them will be a guarantor for that.

68:44 So, (Muhammad), <u>forsake</u> Me and whoever denies this discourse. We will draw them on gradually from where they know not.

68:48 So <u>be</u> **you** <u>patient</u> until the determination of **your** Lord and be not like the Companion of the Great Fish (Jonah) when he cried out, one who is suppressed by grief.

3. Chapter 73: The One Who is Wrapped (al-Muzzammil)
73:2 <u>Stand up</u>, (Muhammad), during the night, but a little part.

73:3 (Or) for half of it or <u>reduce</u> it a little, (Muhammad).

73:4 Or <u>increase</u> it and <u>chant</u> the Quran, a good chanting.

73:8 <u>Remember</u>, (Muhammad), the Name of **your** Lord. Devote **your**self to Him with total devotion.

73:9 The Lord of the East and of the West, there is no god but He. So <u>take</u> Him to **your**self as **your** Trustee.

73:10 <u>Have</u> **you** <u>patience</u> with regard to what they say and <u>abandon</u> them with a graceful abandoning.

73:11 <u>Forsake</u> to Me, (Muhammad), the ones who deny, those imbued with prosperity and respite them for a little.

4. Chapter 74: The One Who Is Wrapped in a Cloak (al-Muddaththir)
74:2 <u>Stand up</u>, (Muhammad), and <u>warn</u>!

74:3 <u>Magnify</u> **your** Lord, (Muhammad),

74:4 <u>Purify</u> **your** garments, (Muhammad).

74:5 <u>Abandon</u> contamination, (Muhammad)!

74:7 For **your** Lord, then, <u>have</u> **you** <u>patience</u>, (Muhammad).

74:11 <u>Leave</u> (Muhammad), Me alone whom I created.

8. CHAPTER 87: THE LOFTY (AL-AALI)

87:1 <u>Glorify</u> the Name of **your** Lord, The Lofty, (Muhammad).

87:9 So <u>remind</u>, (Muhammad), if a reminder profited them.

10. CHAPTER 89: THE DAWN (AL-FAJR)

89:28 <u>Return</u> to **your** Lord, (Muhammad), one that is well-pleasing, well-pleased:

89:29 <u>Enter</u> **you**, (Muhammad), among My servants.

89:30 Enter **you**, (Muhammad), My Garden!

11. CHAPTER 93: THE FORENOON (AL-DUHA)

93:11 As for the divine blessing of **your** Lord, (Muhammad), <u>divulge</u> it!

12. CHAPTER 94: THE EXPANSION (AL-INSHIRAH)

94:7-94:8 When **you** had finished **your** duties, then, <u>work</u> on supplication, and <u>quest</u> **your** Lord.

15. CHAPTER 108: THE ABUNDANCE (AL-KAWTHAR)

108:2 So <u>invoke blessings</u> for **your** Lord and <u>make sacrifice</u>.

23. CHAPTER 53: THE STAR (AL-NAJM)

53:29 So <u>turn</u> **you** <u>aside,</u> (Muhammad), from him who turns away from Our Remembrance and he wants nothing but this present life.

31. CHAPTER 75: THE RESURRECTION (AL-QIYAMAH)

75:18 But when We recited it, <u>follow</u> **you** its Recitation.

34. CHAPTER 50: QAF (QAF)

50:40 In the night <u>glorify</u> Him, (Muhammad), and at the end part of the prostrations.

50:41 <u>Listen</u>, (Muhammad), on a Day when one who calls out will cry out from a near place.

36. CHAPTER 86: THE NIGHT VISITOR (AL-TARIQ)

86:17 So, (Muhammad), <u>respite</u> the ones who are ungrateful! <u>Grant</u> **you** them a <u>delay</u> for a while.

37. CHAPTER 54: THE MOON (AL-QAMAR)

54:6 So <u>turn</u> **you** <u>away</u> from them, (Muhammad), on a Day when One Who Calls will call to a horrible thing.

38. Chapter 38: Saad (Saad)

38:17 <u>Have patience</u>, (Muhammad), with what they say, and <u>remember</u> Our servant David, the possessor of potency. Truly, he was penitent.

38:41 <u>Remember</u> Our servant Job, (Muhammad), when he cried out to his Lord: Truly, Satan afflicted me with fatigue and punishment!

38:48 <u>Remember</u> Ishmael, Elisha, and Dhul Kifl, (Muhammad). All are among the good.

39. Chapter 7: The Elevated Places (al-Araf)

7:84 We rained down a rain on them. So <u>look</u>, (Muhammad), on how had been the Ultimate End of the ones who sin.

7:86 Sit not by every path intimidating and barring from the way of God those who believed in Him and you desire it to be crooked. Remember when you had been few and He augmented you. <u>Look</u>, (Muhammad), on how had been the Ultimate End of the ones who make corruption.

7:87 If there had been a section of you who believed in what I was sent with and a section believe not, <u>have patience</u>, (Muhammad), until God gives judgment between us. He is Best of the ones who judge.

7:103 Again, We raised up Moses after them with Our signs to Pharaoh and his Council, but they did wrong to them. So <u>look</u>, (Muhammad), on how had been the Ultimate End of the ones who make corruption.

7:163 <u>Ask</u> them about the town, (Muhammad)—that which had been bordering the sea—when they disregarded the Sabbath, when their great fish would approach them on the day of the Sabbath, one that was visible on the shore. The day they keep not the Sabbath, they approach them not. Thus, We try them because they had been disobeying.

7:175 <u>Recount</u> to them, (Muhammad), the tiding of him to whom We gave Our signs, but he cast himself off from them. So Satan pursued him then, he had been among the ones who are in error.

7:176 If We willed, We would have exalted him with them, but he inclined towards the earth, and followed his own desires. His parable is like the parable of a dog. If **you** will attack it, it pants. Or if **you** will leave it, it pants. That is the parable of the folk, those who denied Our signs. Then, <u>relate</u>, (Muhammad), these narratives so that perhaps they will reflect.

7:199 <u>Take</u> the extra and <u>command</u> what is honorable, (Muhammad). <u>Turn aside</u> from the ones who are ignorant.

7:200 But if enmity is sown by Satan in **you**, sowing enmity, then, <u>seek refuge</u>, (Muhammad), in God. Truly, He is Hearing, Knowing.

7:204 When the Quran was recited, <u>listen</u> and <u>pay heed</u> so that perhaps you will find mercy.

7:205 <u>Remember</u> **your** Lord in **your**self humbly and with awe, (Muhammad), instead of openly publishing the sayings at the first part of the day and the eventide. Be **you** not among the ones who are heedless.

41. Chapter 36: YaSin (Ya Sin)

36:11 You, (Muhammad), have only warned whoever followed the Remembrance and dreaded The Merciful in the unseen, so give him good tidings of forgiveness and a generous compensation.

36:13 Propound a parable for them, (Muhammad): The Companions of the Town when ones who were sent drew near them.

42. Chapter 25: The Criterion (al-Furqan)

25:9 Look, (Muhammad), on how they propounded for **you** parables for they went astray and are not able to find a way.

25:52 So do not obey the ones who are ungrateful and struggle, (Muhammad), against them thereby with a great struggle.

25:58 (Muhammad), put **your** trust in the Living Who is Undying and glorify His praise. He sufficed to be aware of the impieties of His servants.

25:59 He Who created the heavens and the earth and whatever is between the two in six days, again, He turned His attention to the Throne. The Merciful! Ask Him, (Muhammad), the One Who is Aware.

44. Chapter 19: Mary (Maryam)

19:16 Remember Mary in the Book, (Muhammad), when she went apart from her people to an eastern place.

19:36 Truly, God is my Lord and your Lord, so worship Him. This is a straight path, (Muhammad).

19:38 How well **you** hear, (Muhammad)! How well they will hear! How well **you** perceive on that Day they will approach Us, but today the ones who are unjust are in a clear wandering astray!

19:39 Warn **you** them of the Day of Regret when the command would be decided, (Muhammad). Yet they are heedless and they believe not.

19:41 Remember Abraham in the Book, (Muhammad). Truly, he had been a just person, a Prophet.

19:51 Remember Moses in the Book, (Muhammad). Truly, he had been one who was devoted and he had been a Messenger, a Prophet.

19:54 Remember Ishmael in the Book, (Muhammad). Truly, he had been one who is sincere in his promise, and he had been a Messenger, a Prophet.

19:56 Remember Enoch in the Book, (Muhammad). Truly, he had been a just person, a Prophet.

19:64-19:65 We come forth not but by the command of **your** Lord. To Him belongs whatever is in advance of us and whatever is behind us and whatever is in between that. **Your** Lord had not been forgetful, the Lord of the heavens and the earth, and what is between them! So worship Him, (Muhammad), and maintain **you** patience in His worship. Have **you** known any namesake for Him?

45. CHAPTER 20: TA HA (TA HA)

20:130 So <u>have</u> **you** <u>patience</u> with what they say and glorify the praises of **your** Lord before the coming up of the sun and before sunset and during the nighttime night watch and glorify at the end of the daytime, so that perhaps **you** will be well-pleased.

20:132 <u>Command</u> **your** people to the formal prayer, (Muhammad), and to <u>maintain patience</u> in it. We ask not of **you** for any provision (for Us). We provide for **you** and the Ultimate End will be for the God-conscious.

46. CHAPTER 56: THE INEVITABLE (AL-WAQIAH)

56:74 Then, <u>glorify</u> with the name of **your** Lord, The Sublime, (Muhammad).

56:96 So <u>glorify</u> the Name of **your** Lord, The Almighty, (Muhammad).

47. CHAPTER 26: THE POETS (AL-SHUARA)

26:69 <u>Recount</u> to them the tidings of Abraham, (Muhammad).

26:214 <u>Warn</u> **your** nearest kin, the kinspeople, (Muhammad).

26:215 <u>Make low</u> **your** wing to whoever followed **you** among the ones who believe, (Muhammad).

26:217 <u>Put</u> **your** <u>trust</u> in The Almighty, The Compassionate, (Muhammad).

48. CHAPTER 27: THE ANT (AL-NAML)

27:14 They negated them—although their souls confessed to them—out of injustice and self-exaltation. So <u>look</u>, (Muhammad), on how had been the Ultimate End of the ones who make corruption.

27:51 So <u>look</u>, (Muhammad), on how had been the Ultimate End of their planning! Truly, We destroyed them and their folk one and all.

27:79 So <u>put</u> **your** <u>trust</u> in God, (Muhammad). Truly, **you** are on The Clear Truth.

49. CHAPTER 28: THE STORY (AL-QASAS)

28:50 But if they respond not to **you**, then, <u>know</u>, (Muhammad), that they only follow their own desires. Who is one who goes astray other than whoever followed his own desires without guidance from God? Truly, God guides not the folk, the ones who are unjust.

28:87 Let them not bar **you** from the signs of God after they were caused to descend to **you**. <u>Call</u> to **your** Lord, (Muhammad). Be **you** not among the ones who are polytheists.

50. CHAPTER 17: THE JOURNEY BY NIGHT (AL-ISRA)

17:14 <u>Recite</u> **your** book, (Muhammad)! This day **your** soul sufficed **you** as **your** reckoner against **you**.

17:21 <u>Look,</u> (Muhammad), on how We gave advantage to some of them over some others. Certainly, the world to come will be greater in degrees and greater in excellence.

17:26 (Muhammad), <u>give</u> to the possessor of kinship his right and to the needy and to the traveler of the way. Spend not extravagantly, an extravagant spending.

17:48 <u>Look,</u> (Muhammad), on how they propounded parables for **you**. So they went astray and they are not able to be on a way.

17:61 Mention, (Muhammad), when We said to the angels: <u>Prostrate</u> yourselves to Adam! so they prostrated themselves, but Iblis. He said: Will I prostrate myself to one whom **You** had created from clay?

17:78 <u>Perform</u> the formal prayer, (Muhammad), from the sinking sun until the darkening of the night and the recital at dawn. Truly, the dawn recital had been one that is witnessed.

17:79 <u>Keep vigil</u> with it in the night as a work of supererogation for **you**, (Muhammad). Perhaps **your** Lord will raise **you** up to a station of one who is praised.

17:101 Certainly, We gave Moses nine signs, clear portents. Then, <u>ask</u> the Children of Jacob, (Muhammad), when he drew near them. Then Pharaoh said to him: Truly, O Moses, I think that **you** are one who is bewitched.

51. CHAPTER 10: JONAH (YUNUS)

10:2 These are the signs of the wise Book. Had it been for humanity to wonder that We revealed to a man from among them that: <u>Warn</u> humanity and <u>give</u> **you** <u>good tidings</u> to those who believed, (Muhammad), so that they will have a sound footing with their Lord? The ones who are ungrateful said: Truly, this is one who is a clear sorcerer.

10:39 Nay! They denied the knowledge that they comprehend not while approaches them not the interpretation. Thus, those who were before them denied. So <u>look,</u> (Muhammad), on how had been the Ultimate End of the ones who are unjust!

10:71 <u>Recount</u> to them, (Muhammad), the tidings of Noah when he said to his folk: O my folk! If my station had been troublesome to you and my reminding you of the signs of God, then, in God I put my trust. So summon up your affair along with your ascribed associates. Again, there be no cause for doubt in your affair. Again, decide against me and give me no respite.

10:73 Then, they denied him, so We delivered him and some with him on the boat. We made them the viceregents while We drowned those who denied Our signs. Then, <u>look,</u> (Muhammad), on how had been the Ultimate End of the ones who are warned!

10:105 <u>Set</u> **you your** <u>face,</u> (Muhammad), to the way of life of a monotheist. Be **you** not among the ones who are polytheists.

10:109 <u>Follow</u> **you** what is revealed to **you**, (Muhammad). <u>Have</u> **you** patience until God gives judgment. He is Best of the ones who judge.

52. CHAPTER 11: HUD (HUD)

11:49 That is of the tidings of the unseen that We reveal to **you**, (Muhammad). **You** have not been knowing of them nor thy folk before this. So have **you** patience. Truly, the Ultimate End is for the ones who are Godfearing.

11:112 So go **you** straight, (Muhammad), as **you** were commanded and those who repented with **you** and be not defiant. Truly, He is Seeing of what you do.

11:114 Perform the formal prayer, (Muhammad), at the two ends of the daytime and at nearness of the nighttime. Truly, benevolence causes evil deeds to be put away. That is a reminder for the ones who remember.

11:115 Have **you** patience, (Muhammad), for, truly, God wastes not the compensation of the ones who are doers of good.

11:123 To God belongs the unseen of the heavens and the earth. To Him is the return of every command, so worship Him, (Muhammad), and put **your** trust in Him. **Your** Lord is not One Who is Heedless of what you do.

54. CHAPTER 15: THE ROCKY TRACT (AL-HIJR)

15:3 Forsake them, (Muhammad), to eat and let them take joy and be diverted with hopefulness. Then, they will know.

15:49 Tell My servants, (Muhammad), that I am The Forgiving, The Compassionate.

15:51 Tell them, (Muhammad), about the guests of Abraham.

15:85 We created not the heavens and the earth and whatever is in between them but with The Truth. Truly, the Hour is one that arrives. So, (Muhammad), overlook (forgive), with a graceful overlooking (forgiveness).

15:88 Stretch not out **your** eyes for what We gave of enjoyment in this life to spouses among them, (Muhammad), nor feel remorse for them, but make low **your** wing in kindness to the ones who believe.

15:94 So call aloud what **you** are commanded: Turn aside, (Muhammad), from the ones who are polytheists!

15:98 So glorify the praises of **your** Lord, (Muhammad), and be among the ones who prostrate themselves.

15:99 Worship **your** Lord until the certainty approaches **you**, (Muhammad).

55. CHAPTER 6: THE FLOCKS (AL-ANAM)

6:24 Look, (Muhammad), on how they have lied against themselves. Went astray with them that which they had been devising.

6:51 Warn with the Quran, (Muhammad), those who fear that they will be assembled before their Lord. Other than He there is neither a protector nor an intercessor, so that perhaps they will be Godfearing.

6:68 When **you** had seen those who engage in idle talk about Our signs, then, turn aside, (Muhammad), from them until they discuss in conversation other than that. If Satan should cause **you** to forget, then, after a reminder, sit not with the folk, the ones who are unjust.

6:70 Forsake, (Muhammad), those who took to themselves their way of life as a pastime and as a diversion and whom this present life deluded. But remind with it, the Quran, so that a soul would not be given up to destruction for what it earned. Other than God there is not for it a protector nor an intercessor. Even if it be an equitable equivalent, it will not be taken from it. Those are those who were given up to destruction for what they earned. For them is a drink of scalding water and a painful punishment because they had been ungrateful.

6:90 Those are those whom God guided. So imitate their guidance, (Muhammad). Say: I ask of you no compensation for it. It is not but a reminder for the worlds.

6:106 Follow **you** what was revealed to **you** from **your** Lord, (Muhammad). There is no god but He. Turn **you** aside from the ones who are polytheists.

6:112 Thus, We made an enemy for every Prophet, satans from among humankind and the jinn. Some of them reveal to some others a flashy saying, a delusion. If **your** Lord willed, they would not have accomplished it. So forsake them, (Muhammad), and what they devise.

6:137 Thus, made to appear pleasing to many of the ones who are polytheists was the killing of their children by those whom they ascribe as associates with Him so that they deal them destruction and so that they confuse their way of life for them. If God willed, they would not have accomplished it. So forsake them, (Muhammad), and what they devise.

56. CHAPTER 37: THE ONES STANDING IN RANK (AL-SAFFAT)

37:11 So ask them, (Muhammad), for advice: Are they stronger in constitution or those others whom We created? Truly, We created them of clinging clay.

37:73 Then, (Muhammad), look on how had been the Ultimate End of the ones who are warned.

37:149 Then, (Muhammad), ask them for advice: Are daughters for **your** Lord and for them, sons?

37:174 So turn **you** away from them for awhile, (Muhammad).

37:175 Perceive them, (Muhammad), and soon they will perceive.

37:178 So turn **you** away from them for a while, (Muhammad).

37:179 Perceive , (Muhammad), and they will perceive.

57. CHAPTER 31: LUQMAN (LUQMAN)

31:7 When Our signs are recounted to him, he turned as one who grows arrogant, as if he had not been hearing them, as if there had been heaviness in his ears. So <u>give</u> him, (Muhammad), <u>tidings</u> of a painful punishment.

59. CHAPTER 39: THE TROOPS (AL-ZUMAR)

39:2 Truly, We caused to descend to **you** the Book with The Truth so <u>worship</u> God as one who is sincere and devoted in the way of life to Him.

39:17 Those who avoided false deities so that they worship them not and were penitent to God, for them are good tidings. So <u>give good tidings</u>, (Muhammad), to My servants,

39:66 Nay! <u>Worship</u> **you** God and be **you** among the ones who are thankful!

60. CHAPTER 40: THE ONE WHO FORGIVES (AL-GHAFIR)

40:7 (Muhammad): Those who carry the Throne and whoever is around it glorify the praises of their Lord. They believe in Him and ask for forgiveness for those who believed: Our Lord! **You** had encompassed everything in mercy and in knowledge. So <u>forgive</u> those who repented and who followed **your** way and <u>guard</u> them from the punishment of hellfire.

40:18 <u>Warn</u> them, (Muhammad), of The Impending Day when the hearts will be near the throats, ones who choke. There will not be a loyal friend for ones who are unjust, nor an intercessor be obeyed.

40:55 So <u>have</u> **you** <u>patience</u>, (Muhammad). Truly, the promise of God is true. <u>Ask</u> for forgiveness for **your** impiety. <u>Glorify</u> **your** Lord with praise in the evening and the early morning.

40:56 Truly, those who dispute about the signs of God without any authority having approached them, there is nothing but having pride in their breasts. They will never be ones who reach its satisfaction. So <u>seek refuge</u> in God, (Muhammad). Truly, He, He is The Hearing, The Seeing.

40:77 So <u>have</u> **you** <u>patience</u>, (Muhammad). Truly, the promise of God is true. And whether We cause **you** to see some part of what We promise them or We call **you** to Us, then, it is to Us they will be returned.

61. CHAPTER 41: THEY WERE EXPLAINED DISTINCTLY
(AL-FUSSILAT)

41:34 Not on the same level are benevolence or the evil deed. <u>Drive back</u> with what is fairer, (Muhammad). Then, behold he who between **you** and between him was enmity as if he had been a protector, a loyal friend.

41:36 But if Satan sows enmity, sowing enmity in **you**, then, <u>seek refuge</u> in God, (Muhammad). Truly, He is The Hearing, The Knowing.

63. CHAPTER 43: THE ORNAMENTS (AL-ZUKHRUF)

43:25 So We requited them. Then, <u>look</u>, (Muhammad), on how had been the Ultimate End of the ones who deny.

43:43 So hold **you** fast to what was revealed to **you**, (Muhammad). Truly, **you** are on a straight path.

43:45 Ask ones whom We sent before **you** of Our Messengers, (Muhammad): Made We gods other than the Merciful to be worshiped?

43:83 So leave them to engage in idle talk and play, (Muhammad), until they encounter their Day which they are promised.

64. CHAPTER 44: THE SMOKE (AL-DUKHAN)

44:10 Then, **you** watch for a Day when the heavens will bring a clear smoke, (Muhammad).

44:59 So **you** watch, (Muhammad)! Truly, they are ones who watch.

65. CHAPTER 45: THE ONES WHO KNEEL (AL-JATHIYAH)

45:8 He hears the signs of God being recounted to him. Again, he persists as one who grows arrogant as if he hears them not. So, (Muhammad), give him tidings of a painful punishment!

45:18 Again, We assigned **you**, (Muhammad), an open way of the command so follow it and follow not the desires of those who know not.

66. CHAPTER 46: THE CURVING SANDHILLS (AL-AHQAF)

46:21 Remember, (Muhammad), the brother of Aad when he warned his folk in the curving sandhills. Warnings passed away before and after him saying: Worship nothing but God. Truly, I fear for you the punishment of a tremendous Day.

46:35 So have **you** patience, (Muhammad), as endured patiently those imbued with constancy of the Messengers and let them not seek to hasten the Judgment. As, truly, on a Day they will see what they are promised as if they lingered not in expectation but for an hour of daytime. This is delivering the message! Will any be caused to perish but the folk, the ones who disobey?

67. CHAPTER 15: THE WINNOWING WINDS (AL-DHARIYAT)

51:54 So turn **you** away, (Muhammad), from them that **you** be not one who is reproached.

51:55 Remind, (Muhammad), for, truly, the reminder profits the ones who believe.

68. CHAPTER 88: THE OVERWHELMING EVENT (AL-GHASHIYAH)

88:21 Then, remind, (Muhammad), for **you** are only one who reminds.

69. CHAPTER 18: THE CAVE (AL-KAHF)

18:27 Recount what was revealed to **you**, (Muhammad), from the Book of **your** Lord. There is no one who changes His Words. **You** will never find other than Him, that which is a haven.

18:28 <u>Have</u> **you** <u>patience</u> **your**self, (Muhammad), with those who call to their Lord in the morning and the evening, wanting His Countenance. Let not **your** eyes pass over them wanting the adornment of this present life. Do not obey him whose heart We made neglectful of Our Remembrance and who followed his own desires and whose affair had been excess.

18:32 <u>Propound</u>, (Muhammad), to them the parable of two men: We assigned to one of them two gardens of grapevines and We encircled them with date palm trees and We made crops between them.

18:45 <u>Propound</u>, (Muhammad), for them the parable of this present life: It is like water that We caused to descend from heaven. Then, plants of the earth mingled with it and it becomes straw in the morning that winnows in the winds. God had been over everything One Who is Omnipotent.

70. CHAPTER 16: THE BEE (AL-NAHL)

16:68 **Your** Lord revealed to **you**, (Muhammad), the bee: <u>Take</u> to **your**self houses from the mountains and in the trees and in what they construct.

16:69 Again, <u>eat</u> (f) of all the fruits and <u>insert</u> (f) **your**self submissively into the ways of **your** Lord, (Muhammad). Drink goes forth from their bellies in varying hues, wherein is healing for humanity. Truly, in this is, certainly, a sign for a folk who reflect.

16:98 So when **you**, (Muhammad), had recited the Quran, <u>seek refuge</u> with God from the accursed Satan.

16:123 Again, we revealed to **you** that **you** <u>follow</u> the creed of Abraham—a monotheist. He had not been among the ones who are polytheists.

16:125 <u>Call</u> **you**, (Muhammad), to the way of **your** Lord with wisdom and fairer admonishment. <u>Dispute</u> with them in a way that is fairer. Truly, **your** Lord is He Who is greater in knowledge of whoever went astray from His way. And He is greater in knowledge of the ones who are truly guided.

16:127 <u>Have</u> **you** <u>patience</u>, (Muhammad). **Your** patience is only from God. Feel not remorse over them, nor be **you** troubled about what they plan.

72. CHAPTER 14: ABRAHAM (IBRAHIM)

14:44 <u>Warn</u> humanity, (Muhammad), of a Day the punishment will approach them. So those who did wrong will say: Our Lord! Postpone for us a near term so that we answer **Your** call and follow the Messengers. (The Quranic response): Yet swore you not an oath before that there would be no going back for you?

73. CHAPTER 21: THE PROPHETS (AL-ANBIYA)

21:7 We sent not before **you**, (Muhammad), but men to whom We reveal. Tell the ungrateful to) <u>ask</u> the People of the Remembrance if you (the ungrateful) had not been knowing.

74. CHAPTER 23: THE BELIEVERS (AL-MUMINUN)

23:54 So forsake you, (Muhammad), them for a while in their obstinacy.

23:96 Drive you back evil deeds with what is fairer, (Muhammad). We are greater in knowledge of what they allege.

75. CHAPTER 32: THE PROSTRATION (AL-SAJDAH)

32:30 So turn you aside, (Muhammad), from them (the ungrateful) and wait awhile. Truly they are ones who are waiting awhile.

76. CHAPTER 52: THE MOUNT (AL-TUR)

52:29 So remind, (Muhammad)! You are not, by the divine blessing of your Lord, a soothsayer nor one who is possessed.

52:45 So, (Muhammad), forsake them (the ungrateful) until they encounter their day in which they will be swooning.

52:48 So have you patience, (Muhammad), for the determination of your Lord, for, truly, you are under Our eyes. Glorify the praises of your Lord when you have stood up at the time of dawn,

52:49 Glorify at night and the drawing back of the stars, (Muhammad).

77. CHAPTER 67: THE DOMINION (AL-MULK)

67:3 Who created the seven heavens one on another? You, (Muhammad), have not seen any imperfection in the creation of The Merciful. Then, return your sight! Have you seen any flaw?

67:4 Again,, (Muhammad), return your sight twice again and your sight will turn about to you, one that is dazzled while it is weary.

78. CHAPTER 69: THE REALITY (AL-HAQQAH)

69:52 So glorify the Name of your Lord, The Sublime, (Muhammad).

79. CHAPTER 70: THE STAIRWAYS OF ASCENT (AL-MAARIJ)

70:5 So have you patience, (Muhammad), with a graceful patience.

70:42 So leave them, (Muhammad), to engage in idle talk and play until they encounter the Day of theirs that they are promised.

83. CHAPTER 84: THE SPLITTING OPEN (AL-INSHIQAQ)

84:24 So give them tidings of a painful punishment, (Muhammad).

84. CHAPTER 30: THE ROMANS (AL-RUM)

30:30 So set your face, (Muhammad), towards a way of life as a monotheist. It is the nature originated by God in which He originated humanity. There is no substitution for the creation of God. That is the truth-loving way of life, but most of humanity knows not.

30:38 So <u>give</u> to possessors of kinship rightfully, (Muhammad), and to the needy and to the traveler of the way. That is better for those who want the Countenance of God. Those, they are the ones who prosper.

30:43 So <u>set</u> **your** face to the truth-loving way of life, (Muhammad), before that Day approaches from God and there is no turning back. They will be split up on that Day.

30:50 <u>Look,</u> (Muhammad), on the effects of the mercy of God, how He gives life to the earth after its death! Truly, that! He is One Who Gives Life to the dead and He is Powerful over everything.

30:60 So <u>have</u> **you** <u>patience,</u> (Muhammad). Truly, the promise of God is True. Let not those who are not certain in belief irritate **you.**

85. Chapter 29: The Spider (al-Ankabut)

29:45 <u>Recount</u> what was revealed to **you** of the Book, (Muhammad), and <u>perform</u> the formal prayer. Truly, the formal prayer prohibits depravity and that which is unlawful, and, truly, the remembrance of God is greater. God knows what you craft.

Madinah Chapters

87. Chapter 2: The Cow (al-Baqarah)

2:25 <u>Give good tidings,</u> (Muhammad), to those who believed and did as the ones in accord with morality, that for them will be Gardens beneath which rivers run. Whenever they were provided from there of its fruit as provision they would say: This is what we were provided before. They will be brought it—ones that resemble one another—and in it for them will be purified spouses. They are ones who will dwell in them forever!

2:125 Mention when We made the House a place of spiritual reward for humanity and a place of sanctuary: <u>Take</u> the Station of Abraham to yourselves as a place of prayer, (Muhammad). We made a compact with Abraham, and Ishmael saying that: <u>Purify</u> My House for the ones who circumambulate it, and the ones who cleave to it, and the ones who bow down, and the ones who prostrate themselves.

2:144 Surely, We see the going to and fro of **your** face toward heaven, (Muhammad). Then, We will turn **you** to a direction of formal prayer that **you** will be well pleased with it. Then, <u>turn</u> **your** face to the direction of the Masjid al-Haram. Wherever you had been, turn your faces to its direction. Truly, those who were given the Book know that it is The Truth from their Lord. God is not One Who is Heedless of what they do.

2:149 From wherever **you** had gone forth, then, <u>turn</u> **your** face in the direction of the Masjid al-Haram, (Muhammad). Truly, this is The Truth from **your** Lord. God is not One Who is Heedless of what you do.

2:150 From wherever **you** had gone forth, then, <u>turn</u> **your** face to the di-

rection of the Masjid al-Haram, (Muhammad). Wherever you (believers) had
been, then, turn your faces to the direction of it so that there be no disputation
from humanity against you, but from those of them who did wrong. Dread
them not, then, but dread Me. And I fulfill My divine blessing on you—so
that perhaps you will be truly guided—

2:155 We will, certainly, try you with something of fear and hunger and
diminution of wealth and lives and fruits, and <u>give good tidings</u>, (Muhammad), to the ones who remain steadfast.

2:211 <u>Ask</u> the Children of Jacob, (Muhammad), how many a sign, a clear
portent, We gave them. Whoever substitutes the divine blessing of God after
it drew near him, then, truly, God is Severe in repayment.

88. CHAPTER 8: THE SPOILS OF WAR (AL-ANFAL)

8:57 So if **you**, (Muhammad), have come upon them in war, then, <u>break</u>
them <u>up</u>, whoever is behind them, so that perhaps they will recollect.

8:58 If **you** have feared treachery from a folk,, (Muhammad), then, <u>dis-
solve</u> the relationship with them equally. Truly, God loves not the ones who
are traitors.

8:61 If they tended towards peace, then, tend **you** towards it, (Muhammad), and <u>put **your** trust</u> in God. Truly, He is The Hearing, The Knowing.

8:65 O Prophet! <u>Encourage</u> fighting to the ones who believe. If there be
twenty of you, ones who remain steadfast, they will vanquish two hundred.
If there be a hundred of you, they will vanquish a thousand of those who
were ungrateful because they are a folk who understand not.

89. CHAPTER 3: THE FAMILY OF IMRAN (AL-I IMRAN)

3:21 Truly, those who are ungrateful for the signs of God and kill the
Prophets without right and kill those who command to equity from among
humanity, then, <u>give</u> **you** to them <u>tidings</u> of a painful punishment.

3:159 It is by the mercy of God **you** were gentle with them, (Muhammad). If **you** had been hard, harsh of heart, they would have broken away
from around **you**. So <u>pardon</u> them and <u>ask for forgiveness</u> for them. <u>Take
counsel</u> with them in the affair. But when **you** are resolved, then, <u>put **your**
trust</u> in God. Truly, God loves the ones who put their trust in Him.

90. CHAPTER 33: THE CONFEDERATES (AL-AHZAB)

33:1 O Prophet! <u>Be Godfearing</u> of God and obey not the ones who are
ungrateful and the ones who are hypocrites. Truly, God had been Knowing,
Wise.

33:2 <u>Follow</u> what is revealed to **you**, (Muhammad), from **your** Lord.
Truly, God is Aware of what you had been doing.

33:3 <u>Put **your** trust</u> in God, (Muhammad). God sufficed as a Trustee.

33:37 Mention when **you**, (Muhammad), have said to him to whom God was gracious and to whom **you** were gracious: Hold back **your** spouse to **your**self and be Godfearing of God. But **you** have concealed in **your**self what God is One Who Shows and **you** have dreaded humanity whereas God has a better right that **you** have dreaded Him. So when Zayd satisfied the necessary formality, We gave her to **you** in marriage so that there be no fault for ones who believe in respect of the spouses of their adopted sons when they (m) satisfied the necessary formality. The command of God had been one that is accomplished.

33:47 Give good tidings to the ones who believe, (Muhammad), that for them is a great grace from God.

33:48 Do not obey the ones who are ungrateful, (Muhammad), and the ones who are hypocrites and heed not their annoyance and put **your** trust in God. God sufficed as a Trustee.

92. CHAPTER 4: THE WOMEN (AL-NISA)

4:50 Look, (Muhammad), on how they devise a lie against God; and it sufficed as clear sin.

4:81 They say: Obedience! Then, when they departed from **you**, (Muhammad), a section of them spent the night planning on other than what **you** have said. God records what they spend the night planning. So turn aside from them and put **your** trust in God. And God sufficed as Trustee.

4:84 So fight **you** in the way of God, (Muhammad). **You** are not placed with a burden but for **your**self. Encourage the ones who believe. Perhaps God will limit the might of those who were ungrateful. God is Stauncher in might and Stauncher in making an example.

4:138 Give **you** tidings, (Muhammad), to the ones who are hypocrites that, truly, for them is a painful punishment.

95. CHAPTER 47: THE CURVING SANDHILLS (AL-AHQAF)

47:19 So know **you**, (Muhammad), that there is no god but God and ask forgiveness for **your** impieties and also for the males, ones who believe and the females, ones who believe. God knows your place of turmoil and your place of lodging.

98. CHAPTER 76: THE HUMAN BEING (AL-INSAN)

76:24 So have **you** patience, (Muhammad), for the determination of **your** Lord and do not obey any one of them, not the ones who are perverted nor the ungrateful.

76:25 Remember, (Muhammad), the Name of **your** Lord at early morning dawn and eventide.

76:26 During the night, prostrate **your**self to Him, (Muhammad), and glorify Him a lengthy part of the night.

103. CHAPTER 22: THE PILGRIMAGE (AL-HAJJ)

22:27 <u>Announce</u> to humanity the pilgrimage to Makkah, (Muhammad). They will approach **you** on foot and on every thin camel. They will approach from every deep ravine.

22:34 For every community We assigned devotional acts that they may remember the Name of God over what We provided them of flocks of animals. Your God is One God. Submit to Him, and <u>give</u> **you**, (Muhammad), <u>good tidings</u> to the ones who humble themselves,

22:37 Neither their flesh nor their blood attains to God, rather, God-consciousness from you attains Him. Thus, He caused them to be subservient to you that you magnify God in that He guided you. <u>Give</u> **you**, (Muhammad), <u>good tidings</u> to the ones who are doers of good.

22:67 For every community We assigned devotional acts so that they be ones who perform rites. So let them not bicker with **you**, (Muhammad), in the command. <u>Call</u> **you** to **your** Lord. Truly, **you** are on a guidance, that which is straight.

104. CHAPTER 63: THE HYPOCRITES (AL-MUNAFIQUN)

63:4 When **you**, (Muhammad), have seen them, their physiques impress **you**. When they speak, **you** have heard their saying. It is as if they had been propped up timber. They assume that every Cry is against them. They are the enemy so <u>beware</u> of them. God took the offensive. How they are misled!

107. CHAPTER 66: THE FORBIDDING (AL-TAHRIM)

66:9 O Prophet! <u>Struggle</u> against the ones who are ungrateful and the ones who are hypocrites and <u>be</u> **you** <u>harsh</u> against them. Their place of shelter will be hell. Miserable will be the Homecoming!

109. CHAPTER 61: THE RANKS (AL-SAFF)

61:13 He gives another thing you love, help is from God and victory in the near future, so <u>give good tidings</u>, (Muhammad), to the ones who believe.

112. CHAPTER 5: THE TABLE SPREAD WITH FOOD (AL-MAIDA)

5:13 Then, for their breaking their solemn promise, We cursed them and We made their hearts ones that harden. They tamper with the words out of context and they forgot an allotment of what they were reminded of in it. **You** will not cease to peruse the treachery of them, but a few of them. Then, <u>overlook</u> and <u>pardon</u> them, (Muhammad). Truly, God loves the ones who are doers of good.

5:27 <u>Recount</u> **you** to them, (Muhammad), the tiding of the two sons of Adam in Truth when they both brought near a sacrifice and it was received from one of them but there is non-acceptance from the other. He (Cain) said:

I will, surely, kill **you** (Abel). He (Abel) said: Truly, God receives only from the ones who are Godfearing.

5:42 They are ones who hearken to lies, the ones who devour the wrongful. Then, if they drew near you, then, <u>give</u> **you** <u>judgment</u>, (Muhammad), between them or <u>turn aside</u> from them. If **you** have turned aside from them, then, they will never injure **you** at all. If **you** had given judgment, then, <u>give</u> <u>judgment</u> between them with equity. Truly, God loves the ones who act justly.

5:44 Truly, We caused the Torah to descend wherein is guidance and light. The Prophets give judgment with it, those who submitted to God, for those who became Jews and the rabbis and learned Jewish scholars who committed to memory the Book of God and they had been witnesses to it. So dread not humanity, but <u>dread</u> Me. Exchange not My signs for a little price. Whoever gives not judgment by what God caused to descend, those, they are the ones who are ungrateful.

5:48 We caused the Book to descend to **you**, (Muhammad), with The Truth, that which establishes as true what was before it of the Book and that which preserves it. So <u>give judgment</u> between them by what God caused to descend. Follow not their desires that drew near **you** against The Truth. For each among you We made a divine law and an open road. If God willed, He would have made you one community to try you with what He gave you so be forward in good deeds. To God is your return altogether. Then, He will tell you about what you had been at variance in it.

5:49 <u>Give judgment</u>, (Muhammad), between them by what God caused to descend and follow not their desires and beware of them so that they tempt **you** not from some of what God caused to descend to you. If they turned away, then, know that God only wants that He light on them for some of their impieties. Truly, many within humanity are ones who disobey.

5:67 O Messenger! <u>State</u> what was caused to descend to **you** from **your** Lord, for if **you** have not accomplished it, then, **you** will not have stated His message. God will save **you** from the harm of humanity. Truly, God guides not the folk, the ones who are ungrateful.

5:75 The Messiah son of Mary was not but a Messenger. Surely, Messengers passed away before him. His mother was a just person (f). They both had been eating food. <u>Look</u>, (Muhammad), on how We make manifest the signs to them. Again, <u>look</u> on how they are misled!

113. CHAPTER 9: REPENTANCE (AL-TAWBAH)

9:3 The announcement from God and His Messenger to humanity on the day of the greater pilgrimage to Makkah is that God is free from the ones who are polytheists and so is His Messenger. Then, it will be better for you if you repented. But if you turned away, then, know that you are not ones who frustrate God. <u>Give</u> **you** <u>tidings</u>, (Muhammad), to those who were ungrateful of a painful punishment.

9:6 If anyone of the ones who are polytheists sought asylum with **you**, ,
(Muhammad), then, <u>grant</u> him <u>protection</u> so that he hears the assertions of
God. Again, convey **you** him to a place of safety. That is because they are a
folk who know not.

9:34 O those who believed! Truly, there are many of the learned Jewish
scholars and monks who consume the wealth of humanity in falsehood and
bar from the way of God and those who treasure up gold and silver and spend
it not in the way of God. <u>Give</u> to them, (Muhammad), <u>tidings</u> of a painful
punishment,

9:73 O Prophet! <u>Struggle</u> with the ones who are ungrateful and the ones
who are hypocrites and <u>be</u> **you** <u>harsh</u> against them. Their place of shelter will
be hell. Miserable will be the Homecoming!

9:80 <u>Ask for forgiveness</u> for them, (Muhammad), or ask not for forgiveness for them, if **you** have asked for forgiveness for them seventy times, God
will never forgive them. That is because they were ungrateful to God and His
Messenger. God guides not the folk, the ones who disobey.

9:103 <u>Take</u> charity from their wealth to purify them and make them pure
with it. <u>Invoke blessings</u> for them. Truly, **your** entreaties will bring a sense
of comfort and rest to them. God is Hearing, Knowing.

9:111-9112 Truly, God has bought from the ones who believe themselves
and their properties for the Garden is theirs! They fight in the way of God so
they kill and are slain. It is a promise rightfully on Him in the Torah and the
Gospel and the Quran. Who is more true to His compact than God? Then rejoice in the good tidings of the bargain that you made in the trade with Him.
That, it is the winning the sublime triumph for the repentant worshippers, the
ones who praise, the ones who are inclined to fasting, the ones who bow
down, the ones who prostrate themselves, the ones who command that which
is honorable and the ones who prohibit that which is unlawful, and the ones
who guard the ordinances of God, and <u>give</u> **you** <u>good tidings</u>, (Muhammad),
to the ones who believe!

114. CHAPTER 110: THE HELP (AL-NASR)

110:3 Then, <u>glorify</u> the praise of **your** Lord, (Muhammad), and <u>ask for</u>
His <u>forgiveness</u>. Truly, He had been ever The Accepter of Repentance.

PART 4. OTHER QURANIC COMMANDS ADDRESSED TO HUMANITY (2ND PERSON PLURAL) IN CHRONOLOGICAL ORDER

MAKKAH SIGNS

2. CHAPTER 68: THE PEN (AL-QALAM)
68:22 <u>Set forth</u> in the early morning dawn to your cultivation if you had been ones who pluck fruit.

3. CHAPTER 73: THE ONE WHO IS WRAPPED (AL-MUZZAMMIL)
73:20 Truly, **your** Lord knows that **you** be standing up for nearly two thirds of the nighttime, or a half of it or a third of it along with a section of those who are with **you**. God ordains the nighttime and the daytime. He knew that you would not be able to keep count of it, so He turned towards you in forgiveness, then recite of the Quran as much as was easy. He knew that some of you are sick and others travel on the earth looking for the grace of God and others fight in the way of God. So <u>recite</u> of it as much as was easy. <u>Perform</u> the formal prayer and <u>give</u> the purifying alms and <u>lend</u> to God a fairer loan. For whatever of good you put forward for your souls, you will find the same with God. It is good and a sublime compensation. <u>Ask</u> God <u>for forgiveness</u>. Truly, God is Forgiving, Compassionate.

23. CHAPTER 53: THE STAR (AL-NAJM)
53:62 So <u>prostrate</u> yourselves to God and <u>worship</u> Him.

33. CHAPTER 77: THE ONES WHO ARE SENT (AL-MURASALAT)
77:29 <u>Set out</u> toward what you had been in it denying.
77:30 <u>Set out</u> to the shade. It is possessor of three columns,
77:39 So if you had been cunning, then, <u>try</u> to outwit Me.
77:43 <u>Eat</u> and <u>drink</u> wholesomely for what you had been doing.
77:46 <u>Eat</u>, take joy for a little. You are ones who sin.
77:48 When it will be said: <u>Bow down</u>, they bow not down.

34. CHAPTER 50: QAF (QAF)
50:34 <u>Enter</u> you there in peace. That is the Day of Eternity!

37. CHAPTER 54: THE MOON (AL-QAMAR)
54:48 On a Day they (the ungrateful) will be dragged into the fire on their faces: <u>Experience</u> the touch of Saqar!

38. Chapter 38: Saad (Saad)

38:6 The Council set out from them, saying: Be gone! Have patience with your gods. Truly, this is a thing to be wanted!

39. Chapter 7: The Elevated Places (al-Araf)

7:3 Follow what was caused to descend to you from your Lord and follow not protectors other than He. Little you recollect!

7:31 O Children of Adam! Take your adornment at every place of prostration. Eat and drink, but exceed not all bounds. Truly, He loves not the ones who are excessive.

7:39 The first of them would say to the last of them: You have had no superiority over us so experience the punishment for what you had been earning.

7:49 Are these, those about whom you swore an oath that God would never impart mercy? Enter the Garden. There will be neither fear in you nor will you feel remorse.

7:55 Call to your Lord humbly and inwardly. Truly, He loves not the ones who exceed the limits.

7:56 Do not make corruption in the earth after things were made right and call to Him with fear and hope. Truly, the mercy of God is Near to the ones who are doers of good.

7:180 To God belongs the Fairer Names, so call to Him by them. Forsake those who blaspheme His Names. They will be given recompense for what they had been doing.

7:194 Truly, those whom you call to other than God are servants like you. So call to them and let them respond to you if you had been ones who are sincere.

41. Chapter 36: YaSin (Ya Sin)

36:59 Be separated on this Day, O ones who sin!

36:61 Worship you Me. This is a straight path.

36:64 Roast in it this Day because you had been ungrateful.

42. Chapter 25: The Criterion (al-Furqan)

25:14 It will be said to them: Call you not today for a single damnation, but call for many damnations!

25:60 When it was said to them: Prostrate yourselves to The Merciful, they said: What is The Merciful? Will we prostrate ourselves to what thou hast commanded us? It increased aversion in them.

43. Chapter 35: The Originator (al-Fatir)

35:3 O humanity! Remember the divine blessing of God on you! Is there anyone who is a creator other than God Who provides for you from the heaven and the earth? There is no god but He. Then, how you are misled!

35:6 Truly, Satan is an enemy to you so <u>take</u> him to yourselves as an enemy. He calls only his party that they be among the Companions of the Blaze.

35:40 Say: Considered you yourselves ascribed associates to whom you call to other than God? <u>Cause me to see</u> what they created in the earth or have they any association in creation of the heavens? Or gave We them a Book so that they have a clear portent from there? Nay! The ones who are unjust promise nothing—some of them to some others—but delusion.

45. Chapter 20: Ta Ha (Ta Ha)
20:135 Say: Each is one who is waiting so <u>watch</u>. Then, you will know who are the Companions of the Path without fault and who were truly guided.

48. Chapter 27: The Ant (al-Naml)
27:64 Who begins creation, again, will cause it to return and Who provides you from the heaven and the earth. Is there a god besides God? Say: <u>Prepare</u> your <u>proof</u> (ungrateful) if you had been ones who are sincere!

27:69 Say: <u>Journey</u> through the earth; then, <u>look</u> on how had been the Ultimate End of the ones who sin.

49. Chapter 28: The Story (al-Qasas)
28:49 Say: Then, <u>bring</u> a Book from God that is better guided than these two that I follow it, if you had been ones who are sincere.

28:64 It would be said (to the ungrateful): <u>Call</u> to your ascribed associates. Then, they will call to them, but they will not respond to them and they will see the punishment. If only they had been truly guided!

28:75 We will tear out a witness from every community and We will say: <u>Prepare</u> your <u>proof</u>. Then, they will know that The Truth is with God and will go astray from them what they had been devising.

50. Chapter 17: The Journey by Night (al-Isra)
17:34 Come not near the property of the orphan, but with what is fairer until he reaches the coming of age. <u>Live up</u> to the compact. Truly, the compact had been that which will be asked about.

17:35 <u>Live up</u> to the full measure when you wanted to measure. And <u>weigh</u> with a scale, one that is straight. That is best and fairer in interpretation.

17:56 Say: <u>Call</u> (you ungrateful) to those whom you claimed other than Him. Then, they are neither in control to remove harm from you nor revise it.

17:107 Say: <u>Believe</u> in it (ungrateful) or believe not. Truly, those who were given the knowledge before it, when it is recounted to them, they fall down on their faces, ones who prostrate.

17:110 Say: Call to God or call to the Merciful. By whatever you call Him, to Him are the Fairer Names. Be **you** not loud in thy formal prayer nor speak in a low tone and look for a way between.

51. CHAPTER 10: JONAH (YUNUS)

10:3 Truly, your Lord is God Who created the heavens and the earth in six days. Again, He turned Himself to the Throne managing the command. There is no intercessor but after His permission. That is God, your Lord, so worship Him alone. Will you not, then, recollect?

10:20 They say: Why was a sign not caused to descend from his Lord? Say: Truly, the unseen belongs only to God. So wait awhile. Truly, I am with you of the ones who are waiting awhile.

10:38 Or they will say: He devised it. Say (to the ungrateful): Bring a Chapter of the Quran like it and call to whomever you were able—other than God—if you had been ones who are sincere.

10:52 Again, it would be said to those who did wrong: Experience the infinite punishment! Will you be given recompense but for what you had been earning?

10:101 Say: Look on what is in the heavens and the earth. Neither the signs nor the warning avail a folk who believe not.

10:102 So wait they awhile but like in the days of those who passed away before them? Say: So wait awhile. I am with you among the ones waiting awhile!

52. CHAPTER 11: HUD (HUD)

11:3 Ask for forgiveness from your Lord. Again, repent to Him that He give you fairer enjoyment for a term that which is determined. He gives His grace to every possessor of grace. If they turn away, I fear for you the punishment of a Great Day.

11:13 Say: Approach you (ungrateful), then, with ten chapters of the Quran like it, that which is forged, and call to whomever you were able other than God if you had been ones who are sincere.

11:14 If they respond not to you, then, know that it was only caused to descend by the knowledge of God and that there is no god but He. Are you, you, then, ones who submit to God?

11:121 Say to those who believe not: Act according to your ability. Truly, we are ones who act.

11:122 Wait awhile. We, too, are ones who are waiting awhile.

54. CHAPTER 15: THE ROCKY TRACT (AL-HIJR)

15:46 Enter them in peace as ones who are safe!

55. CHAPTER 6: THE FLOCKS (AL-ANAM)

6:11 Say: Journey through the earth; again, look on how had been the Ultimate End of the ones who deny.

6:30 If **you** would see when they would be stationed before their Lord. He would say: Is this not The Truth? They would say: Yea, by Our Lord. He would say: Then, experience the punishment for what you had been ungrateful.

6:72 Perform the formal prayer and be Godfearing of Him. It is He to Whom you will be assembled.

6:99 It is He Who caused to descend water from heaven. Then, We brought out from it every kind of bringing forth. Then, We brought out herbs from it. We bring out from it thick-clustered grain and from the date palm tree, from the spathe of it, thick clusters of dates, that which draws near and gardens of the grapevines and the olives and the pomegranates, like each to each and not resembling one another. Look on its fruit when it bore fruit and its ripening. Truly, in this are signs for a folk who believe.

6:102 That is God, your Lord. There is no god but He—the One Who is Creator of everything—so worship Him. For He is Trustee over everything.

6:118 So eat of that over which the Name of God was remembered if you had been ones who believe in His signs.

6:120 Forsake manifest sin and its inward part. Truly, those who earn sin, they will be given recompense for what they had been gaining.

6:135 Say: O my folk! Act according to your ability. Truly, I too am one who acts. Then, you will know for whom the Ultimate End will be the abode. Truly, the ones who are unjust will not prosper.

6:141 It is He Who caused gardens to grow, trellised and without being trellised and the date palm trees and a variety of harvest crops and the olives and the pomegranates resembling and not resembling one another. Eat of its fruit when it bore fruit and give its due on the day of its reaping and exceed not all bounds. Truly, He loves not the ones who are excessive.

6:142 Of the flocks are some as beasts of burden and some for slaughter. Eat of what God provided you and follow not in the steps of Satan. Truly, he is a clear enemy to you.

6:143 Eight diverse pairs; two of sheep and two of goats. Say: Forbade He the two males or the two females? Or what is contained in the wombs of the two females? Tell me with knowledge if you had been ones who are sincere.

6:150 Say: Come on! Bring your witnesses who bear witness that God forbade this. Then, if they bore witness, bear you not witness with them. Follow **you** not the desires of those who denied Our signs and those who believe not in the world to come and they equate others with their Lord.

6:152 Come not near the property of the orphan but with what is fairer until one reaches the coming of age. Live up to the full measure and balance with equity. We will not place a burden on any soul, but to its capacity. When you have said something, <u>be just</u>, even if it had been with possessors of kinship and <u>live up</u> to the compact of God. Thus, He charged you with it so that perhaps you will recollect.

6:153 This is My straight path, so <u>follow</u> it. Follow not the ways that will split you up from His way. He charged you this with it, so that perhaps you will be Godfearing.

6:155 This Book We caused to descend is that which is blessed so <u>follow</u> it and <u>be Godfearing</u> so that perhaps you will find mercy.

6:158 Look they on only that the angels approach them? Or **your** Lord approach them? Or some signs of **your** Lord approach them? On a Day that approach some signs of **your** Lord, belief will not profit a person if he believed not before, nor earned good because of his belief. Say: <u>Wait</u> awhile! We too are ones who are waiting awhile!

56. Chapter 37: The Ones Standing in Rank (al-Saffat)

37:22-37:24 <u>Assemble</u> those who did wrong and their spouses, and what they had been worshipping—other than God—and <u>guide</u> them to the path to hellfire. <u>Stop</u> them for they are ones who will be asked.

37:157 Then, <u>bring</u> your Book if you would be ones who are sincere.

57. Chapter 31: Luqman (Luqman)

31:11 This is the creation of God. Then, <u>cause me to see</u> what other than He created? Nay! The ones who are unjust are clearly wandering astray.

31:21 When it was said to them: <u>Follow</u> what God caused to descend. They said: Nay! We will follow what we found our fathers on. Even if it Satan had been calling them to the punishment of the blaze?

31:33 O humanity! <u>Be Godfearing</u> of your Lord, and <u>dread</u> a Day when recompense will not be given by a child to one to whom the child is born, nor will one to whom a child is born be one who gives recompense for the one who is born at all. Truly, the promise of God is True so let not this present life delude you nor let the deluder delude you about God.

58. Chapter 34: Sheba (al-Saba)

34:22 Say: <u>Call on</u> those whom you claimed other than God. They possess not the weight of an atom in the heavens nor on the earth, nor have they in either any association, nor among them is there any sustainer of Him.

34:27 Say: <u>Cause me to see</u> those whom you caused to join with Him as ascribed associates. No indeed! Nay! He is God, The Almighty, The Wise.

34:42 Then, today none of you will possess the power over some others to profit nor hurt and We will say to those who did wrong: <u>Experience</u> the punishment of the fire which you had been denying.

59. CHAPTER 39: THE TROOPS (AL-ZUMAR)

39:15 So <u>worship</u> what you would other than Him. Say: Truly, the ones who are losers are those who lost themselves and their people on the Day of Resurrection. Truly, that is a clear loss.

39:16 They will have overshadowings above from the fire and beneath them, overshadowings. With that, God frightens His servants. O my servants! <u>Be Godfearing</u> of Me!

39:24 Is he, then, one who fends off a dire punishment with his face on the Day of Resurrection? It will be said to the ones who are unjust: <u>Experience</u> what you had been earning!

39:39 Say: O my folk! Truly, <u>act according to your ability</u>. I am one who acts. You will know.

39:54 <u>Be penitent</u> to your Lord and <u>submit</u> to Him before the punishment approaches you. Again, you will not be helped.

39:55 <u>Follow</u> the fairer of what was caused to descend to you from your Lord before the punishment approaches you suddenly while you are not aware.

39:72 It will be said: <u>Enter</u> the doors of hell as ones who will dwell in it forever. Miserable it will be as a place of lodging for the ones who increase in pride.

39:73 Those who were Godfearing will be ones driven to their Lord in the Garden in troops until when they drew near it and its doors were let loose, ones who are its keepers will say to them: Peace be on you! You fared well! So <u>enter</u> it, ones who dwell in it forever.

60. CHAPTER 40: THE ONE WHO FORGIVES (AL-GHAFIR)

40:14 So <u>call</u> you on God ones who are sincere and devoted in the way of life to Him although the ones who are ungrateful disliked it.

40:60 Your Lord said: <u>Call</u> to Me; I will respond to you. Truly, those who grow arrogant toward My worship, they will enter hell as ones who are in a state of lowliness.

40:65 He is The Living! There is no god but He! So <u>call</u> to Him, ones sincere and devoted in the way of life to Him. The Praise belongs to God, the Lord of the worlds!

40:76 <u>Enter</u> the doors of hell as ones who will dwell in it forever. Then, miserable it will be as a place of lodging for the ones who increase in pride!

61. CHAPTER 41: THEY WERE EXPLAINED DISTINCTLY (AL-FUSSILAT)

41:6 Say: I am only a mortal like you. It is revealed to me that your God is God, One; so <u>go straight</u> to Him and <u>ask for forgiveness</u> from Him, and woe to the ones who are polytheists—those who give not the purifying alms

41:26 Those who are ungrateful said: Hear not this, the Quran, but <u>talk</u>

idly about it while it is being recited so that perhaps you will prevail.

41:30 Truly, those who said: Our Lord is God, again, they went straight, the angels come forth to them: Neither fear nor feel remorse, but rejoice in the Gardens which you had been promised.

41:37 Of His signs are the nighttime and the daytime and the sun and the moon. Prostrate not yourselves to the sun nor to the moon, but prostrate yourselves to God Who created both of them if it is He you had been worshiping.

41:40 Truly, those who blaspheme Our signs are not hidden from Us. Is he who is cast down into the fire better off, or he who approaches as one who is safe on the Day of Resurrection? Do as you willed. Truly, He is Seeing of what you do.

62. Chapter 42: The Consultation (al-Shura)

42:13 He laid down the law of the way of life for you, that with which He charged Noah and what We revealed to **you** and that with which We charged Abraham and Moses and Jesus. Perform the prescribed way of life and be not split up in it. Troublesome for the ones who are polytheists is that to which **you** have called them. God elects for Himself whomever He wills and guides the penitent to Himself.

42:47 Respond to the call of your Lord before a Day approaches for which there is no turning back from God. There will be no shelter for you on that Day, nor is there for you any refusal.

63. Chapter 43: The Ornaments (al-Zukhruf)

43:70 Enter the Garden, you and your spouses, to be walking with joy!

64. Chapter 44: The Smoke (al-Dukhan)

44:36 Then, bring our fathers back if you had been ones who are sincere.

44:47 It will be said: Take him and drag him violently into the depths of hellfire.

44:48 Again, then, unloose over his head the punishment of scalding water!

66. Chapter 46: The Curving Sandhills (al-Ahqaf)

46:4 Say: Considered you what you call to other than God? Cause me to see what of the earth they created. Have they an association in the heavens? Bring me a Book from before this, or a vestige of knowledge if you had been ones who are sincere.

46:29 When We turned away from **you** groups of men or jinn who listen to the Quran, when they found themselves in its presence, they said: Pay heed. When it was finished, they turned to their folk, ones who warn.

46:31 O our folk! <u>Answer</u> one who calls to God and <u>believe</u> in Him. He will forgive you your impieties and will grant protection to you from a painful punishment.

46:34 On a Day when will be presented those who were ungrateful to the fire saying: Is not this The Truth? They would say: Yea! By our Lord! He will say: Then, <u>experience</u> the punishment because you had been ungrateful!

67. CHAPTER 15: THE WINNOWING WINDS (AL-DHARIYAT)

51:14 <u>Experience</u> your test. This is that for which you had been seeking to hasten.

51:50 So <u>run away</u> towards God. Truly, I am to you a clear warner from Him.

69. CHAPTER 18: THE CAVE (AL-KAHF)

18:52 On a Day when He will say: <u>Cry out</u> to My associates, those who you claimed. Then, they will call out to them, but they will not respond to them and We will make a gulf of doom between them.

70. CHAPTER 16: THE BEE (AL-NAHL)

16:2 He sends down the angels with the Spirit of His command on whom He wills of His servants: Warn that there is no god but I, so <u>be Godfearing</u> of Me.

16:29 So <u>enter</u> the doors of hell—ones who will dwell in it forever; and, certainly, it will be a miserable place of lodging. It is for the ones who increase in pride!

16:32 Those whom the angels call to themselves while they are ones who are good. They say to them: Peace be unto you! <u>Enter</u> the Garden because of what you had been doing.

16:36 Certainly, We raised up in every community a Messenger saying: <u>Worship</u> God and <u>avoid</u> false deities. Then, of them were some whom God guided and of them were some upon whom their fallacy was realized. So <u>journey</u> through the earth; then, look on how had been the Ultimate End of the ones who deny.

16:43 We sent not before **you** but men to whom We reveal revelation. So <u>ask</u> the People of Remembrance if you had not been knowing.

16:51 God said: Take not two gods to yourselves. Truly, He is One God. Then, <u>have reverence</u> for Me.

16:91 <u>Live up</u> to the compact of God when you have made a contract. Break not the oaths after ratification. Surely, you made God surety over you. Truly, God knows what you accomplish.

16:114 So <u>eat</u> of what God provided you as lawful, what is good and <u>give thanks</u> for the divine blessing of God if it had been Him that you worship.

16:126 If you chastised, then, <u>chastise</u> with the like of that with which you were chastised. But if you endured patiently, certainly, it is better for the ones who remain steadfast.

72. CHAPTER 14: ABRAHAM (IBRAHIM)
14:30 They made rivals with God, causing others to go astray from His way. Say: <u>Take joy</u>, but, truly, your homecoming is the fire!

73. CHAPTER 21: THE PROPHETS (AL-ANBIYA)
21:25 We sent not before **you** any Messenger, but We reveal to him that there is no god but I, so <u>worship</u> Me.

74. CHAPTER 23: THE BELIEVERS (AL-MUMINUN)
23:51 O you Messengers! <u>Eat</u> of what is good and do as one in accord with morality. Truly, I am Knowing of what you do.

23:52 Truly, this, your community is one community and I am your Lord so <u>be Godfearing</u>.

75. CHAPTER 32: THE PROSTRATION (AL-SAJDAH)
32:14 Then, <u>experience</u> it. As you forgot the meeting of this Day of yours, truly, We forgot you. <u>Experience</u> the infinite punishment for what you had been doing.

76. CHAPTER 52: THE MOUNT (AL-TUR)
52:16 <u>Roast</u> you in it! Then, <u>have patience</u>, or you endure patiently not, it is all the same to you. You will be only given recompense for what you had been doing.

52:19 <u>Eat</u> and <u>drink</u> wholesomely because of what you had been doing.

77. CHAPTER 67: THE DOMINION (AL-MULK)
67:13 <u>Keep</u> your saying <u>secret</u> or <u>publish</u> it, truly, He is Knowing of what is in your breasts.

67:15 It is He who made the earth submissive to you, so <u>walk</u> in its tracts and <u>eat</u> of His provision. To Him is the rising.

78. CHAPTER 69: THE REALITY (AL-HAQQAH)
69:24 <u>Eat</u> and <u>drink</u> wholesomely for what you did in the past, in the days, that which have gone by.

69:30 It will be said: <u>Take</u> him and <u>restrict</u> him.

69:31 Again, <u>broil</u> him in hellfire.

69:32 After that in a chain of the length of seventy cubits. So <u>insert</u> him in it.

80. Chapter 78: The Tiding (al-Naba)

78:30 <u>Experience</u> it! We will never increase you but in punishment.

84. Chapter 30: The Romans (al-Rum)

30:31 Be ones who turn in repentance to Him and <u>be Godfearing</u> and <u>perform</u> the formal prayer and be not among the ones who are polytheists.

30:34 They are ungrateful for what We gave them. Then, <u>take joy</u>. You will know.

30:42 Say: <u>Journey</u> through the earth. Then, <u>look</u> on how had been the Ultimate End of those who were before. Most of them had been ones who are polytheists.

85. Chapter 29: The Spider (al-Ankabut)

29:12 Those who are ungrateful said to those wo have believed: <u>Follow</u> our way and we will certainly <u>carry</u> your transgressions while they are not ones who carry any of their own transgressions. Truly, they are the ones who lie.

29:46 Dispute not with the People of the Book unless in a way that is fairer, but with those who did wrong among them. <u>Say</u>: We have believed in what was caused to descend to us and was caused to descend to you and our God and your God is One and we are ones who submit to Him.

29:55 On a Day when the punishment overcomes them from above them and from beneath their feet, He will say: <u>Experience</u> what you had been doing!

Madinah Chapters

87. Chapter 2: The Cow (al-Baqarah)

2:13 When it was said to them: <u>Believe</u> as humanity believed, they said: Will we believe as the fools believed? No! Truly, they, they are the fools, except they know not.

2:21 O humanity! <u>Worship</u> your Lord Who created you and those who were before you so that perhaps you will be Godfearing.

2:23 If you had been in doubt about what We sent down to Our servant, then <u>approach</u> with a Chapter of the Quran —the like of it— and call to your witnesses other than God if you had been ones who are sincere.

2:24 If you accomplish it not —and you will never accomplish it— then <u>be Godfearing</u> of the fire whose fuel is humanity and rocks, prepared for the ones who are ungrateful.

2:104 O those who believed! Say not: Look at us, but say: Wait for us patiently and hear. For the ones who are ungrateful, there is a painful punishment.

2:109 Many of the People of the Book wished that after your belief they return you to being one who is ungrateful out of jealousy within themselves even after The Truth became clear to them. So pardon and overlook them until God brings His command. Truly, God is Powerful over everything.

2:110 Perform the formal prayer and give the purifying alms. Whatever good you put forward for yourselves, you will find it with God. Truly, God is Seeing of what you do.

2:136 Say: We believed in God and what was caused to descend to us, and what was caused to descend to Abraham and Ishmael and Isaac and Jacob and the Tribes and whatever was given Moses and Jesus, and whatever was given to the Prophets from their Lord. We separate and divide not between anyone of them. We are ones who submit to Him.

2:144 Surely, We see the going to and fro of **your** face toward heaven. Then, We will turn **you** to a direction of formal prayer that **you** will be well pleased with it. Then, turn **your** face to the direction of the Masjid al-Haram. Wherever you had been, turn your faces to its direction. Truly, those who were given the Book know that it is The Truth from their Lord, and God is not One Who is Heedless of what they do.

2:148 Everyone has a direction to that which he turns. Be forward, then, in good deeds. Wherever you be, God will bring you altogether for the Judgment. Truly, God is Powerful over everything.

2:150 From wherever **you** had gone forth, then, turn **your** face to the direction of the Masjid al-Haram. Wherever you had been, then, turn your faces to the direction of it so that there be no disputation from humanity against you, but from those of them who did wrong. Dread them not, then, but dread Me. I fulfill My divine blessing on you—so that perhaps you will be truly guided—

2:152 So remember Me and I will remember you. And give thanks to Me, and be not ungrateful!

2:153 O those who believed! Pray for help with patience and formal prayer. Truly, God is with the ones who remain steadfast.

2:167 Those who were followed said: If there be a return again for us, then, we would clear ourselves from them as they cleared themselves from us. Thus, God will cause them to see their actions with regret for them, and they will never be ones who go forth from the fire.

2:168 O humanity! Eat of what is in and on the earth—lawful, wholesome—and follow not the steps of the Satan. Truly, he is a clear enemy to you.

2:170 When it was said to them: Follow what God caused to descend. They said: Nay! We will follow whatever we discovered our fathers were following on it —even though their fathers had been not at all reasonable—

nor are they truly guided.

2:172 O those who believed! Eat of what is good that We provided you
and give thanks to God if it had been He alone whom you worship.

2:187 It is permitted for you on the nights of formal fasting to have sexual intercourse with your wives. They (f) are a garment for you and you are
a garment for them (f). God knew that you had been dishonest to yourselves
so He turned to you in forgiveness and pardoned you. So now lie with them
(f) and look for what God prescribed for you. Eat and drink until the white
thread becomes clear to you from the black thread at dawn. Again, fulfill the
formal fasting until night. Lie not with them (f) when you are ones who
cleave to the places of prostration. These are the ordinances of God. Then,
come not near them. Thus, God makes His signs manifest to humanity so
that perhaps they will be Godfearing.

2:189 They ask **you** about the new moons. Say: They are appointed times
for humanity, and the pilgrimage to Makkah. It is not virtuous conduct that
you approach houses from the back. Rather, virtuous conduct was to be Godfearing, and approach houses from their front doors. Be Godfearing of God
so that perhaps you will prosper.

2:190 Fight in the Way of God those who fight you, but exceed not the
limits. Truly, God loves not the ones who exceed the limits.

2:191 Kill them wherever you came upon them. Drive them out from
wherever they drove you out. Persecution is more grave than killing. Fight
them not near the Masjid al-Haram unless they fight you in it. But if they
fought you, then kill them. Thus, this is the recompense for the ones who are
ungrateful.

2:193-2:200 Fight them until there be no persecution, and the way of
life be for God. Then, if they refrained themselves, then, there is to be no
deep seated dislike, but against the ones who are unjust. Fight aggression
committed in the Sacred Month, in the Sacred Month and so reciprocation
for all sacred things. So whoever exceeded the limits against you, exceed you
the limits against him likewise as he exceeded the limits against you? Be
Godfearing of God and know that God is with the ones who are Godfearing.
Spend in the way of God, and cast not yourselves by your own hands into
deprivation by fighting. Do good. Truly, God loves the ones who are doers
of good. Fulfill the pilgrimage to Makkah, and the visit for God. If you were
restrained, then, whatever was feasible of sacrificial gifts. Shave not your
heads until the sacrificial gift reaches its place of sacrifice. Then, whoever
had been sick among you, or has an injury of his head, then, a redemption of
formal fasting, or charity or a ritual sacrifice. When you were safe, then, whoever took joy in the visit and the pilgrimage to Makkah then whatever was
feasible of a sacrificial gift. Then, whoever finds not the means, then, formal
fasting for three days during the pilgrimage to Makkah and seven when you
returned, that is ten completely. That would be for he whose people are not
ones who are present at the Masjid al-Haram. Be Godfearing of God and

<u>know</u> that God is Severe in repayment.

2:197 The pilgrimage to Makkah is in known months. Whoever under-
took the duty of pilgrimage to Makkah in them, then, there is no sexual intercourse nor disobedience nor dispute during the pilgrimage to Makkah.
Whatever good you accomplish, God knows it. <u>Take</u> provision. Then, truly,
the best ration is God-consciousness. So <u>be Godfearing</u>, O those imbued with
intuition!

2:198 There is no blame on you that you be looking for grace from your
Lord. When you pressed on from Arafat, then <u>remember</u> God at the Sacred
Monument. <u>Remember</u> Him as He guided you, although you had been before
this, certainly, of the ones who go astray.

2:199 Again, <u>press on</u> from where humanity pressed on, and <u>ask</u> God
<u>for forgiveness</u>. Truly, God is Forgiving, Compassionate.

2:200 When you satisfied your devotional acts, then, <u>remember</u> God like
your remembrance of your fathers, or a stauncher remembrance. Among humanity are some who say: Our Lord! <u>Give</u> to us in the present! For him, there
is no apportionment in the world to come!

2:203 <u>Remember</u> God during numbered days. So whoever hastened on
in two days, then, there is no sin on him. Whoever remained behind, then,
there is no sin on him. For whoever was Godfearing, <u>be Godfearing</u> of God.
<u>Know</u> that to Him you will be assembled.

2:208 O those who believed! <u>Enter</u> into peacefulness collectively and
follow not the steps of Satan. Truly, he is a clear enemy to you.

2:209 But if you slipped after drew near you the clear portents, then,
<u>know</u> that God is Almighty, Wise.

2:222 They ask **you** about menstruation. Say: It is an impurity, so <u>with-
draw</u> from your wives during menstruation. Come not near them (f) until
they cleanse themselves. Then, when they (f) cleansed themselves, <u>approach</u>
them (f) as God commanded you. Truly, God loves the contrite and He loves
the ones who cleanse themselves.

2:223 Your wives are a place of cultivation for you, so <u>approach</u> your
cultivation whenever you willed and <u>put forward</u> for yourselves. <u>Be God-
fearing</u> of God. <u>Know</u> that you will be one who encounters Him. Give **you**
good tidings to the ones who believe.

2:231 When you divorced wives, and they (f) reached their (f) term, then,
<u>hold</u> them (f) back as one who is honorable or <u>set</u> them (f) <u>free</u> as one who
is honorable. But hold them (f) not back by injuring them so that you commit
aggression. And whoever commits that, then, surely, he did wrong himself.
And take not to yourselves the signs of God in mockery. <u>Remember</u> the divine blessing of God on you, and what He caused to descend to you from the
Book and wisdom. He admonishes you with it. <u>Be Godfearing</u> of God and
know that God is Knowing of everything.

2:233 The ones who are mothers will breast feed their (f) children for

two years completely for whoever wanted to fulfill breast feeding. On one to
whom a child is born is their (f) provision and their clothing (f) as one who
is honorable. No soul is placed with a burden, but to its capacity. Neither the
one who is a mother be pressed for her child, nor the one to whom a child is
born for his child. On one who inherits is the like of that. While if they both
wanted weaning by them agreeing together and after consultation, then, there
is no blame on either of them. If you wanted to seek wet-nursing for your
children, then, there is no blame on you when you handed over what you
gave as one who is honorable. Be Godfearing of God. Know that God is Seeing of what you do.

2:235-2:236 There is no blame on you in what you offered with it of a
proposal to women, or for what you hid in yourselves. God knew that you
will remember them (f), except appoint not with them (f) secretly, unless you
say a saying as one who is honorable. Resolve not on the knot of marriage
until she reaches her prescribed term. Know that God knows what is within
yourselves. So be fearful of Him. Know that God is Forgiving, Forbearing.
There is no blame on you if you divorced wives whom you touch not, nor
undertake a duty to them (f) of a dowry portion. Make provision for them
(f). For the one who is wealthy—according to his means—and for the one
who is needy—according to his means—with a sustenance, one that is honorable, an obligation on the ones who are doers of good.

2:238 Be watchful of the formal prayers and the middle formal prayer.
Stand up as ones who are morally obligated to God.

2:239 If you feared, then, pray on foot or as one who is mounted. When
you were safe, then, remember God, for He taught you what you be not knowing.

2:243 Have you not considered those who went forth from their abodes
while they were in the thousands being fearful of death? God said to them:
Die! Again, He gave them life. Truly, God is Possessor of Grace for humanity
except most of humanity gives not thanks.

2:244 So fight in the Way of God. Know that God is Hearing, Knowing.

2:254 O those who believed! Spend of what We provided you, before a
Day approaches when there is neither trading in it nor friendship nor intercession. The ones who are ungrateful, they are the ones who are unjust.

2:267 O those who believed! Spend of what is good that you earned, and
from what We brought out for you from the earth. Aim not at getting the bad
of it to spend while you would not be ones who take it, but you would close
an eye to it. Know that God is Sufficient, Worthy of Praise.

2:278 O those who believed! Be Godfearing of God. Forsake what remained of usury, if you had been ones who believe.

2:279 But if you accomplish it not, then, give ear to war from God and
His Messenger. If you repented, you will have your principal capital, doing
no wrong to others nor will you be wronged.

2:281 <u>Be Godfearing</u> of a Day on which you are returned to God. Again, every soul will be paid its account in full for what it earned, and they will not be wronged.

2:282 O those who believed! When you contracted a debt for a term—that which is determined—then, <u>write it down</u>. Let one who is a scribe write it down between you justly. One who is a scribe should not refuse to write it down as God taught him. So let him write down and let the debtor dictate. Let him be Godfearing of God, his Lord, and diminish not anything out of it. But if the debtor had been mentally deficient, or weak, or not able to dictate himself, then, let his protector dictate justly. Call two witnesses to bear witness from among your men. Or if there are not two men, then a man and two women, with whom you are well-pleased as witnesses, so that if one of them (f) goes astray, then, the other one of the two will remind her. The witnesses will not refuse when they were called. Grow not weary that you write it down, be it small or great, with its term. That is more equitable with God and more upright for testimony, and likelier not to be in doubt unless it be a trade, that which is transferred at the time—to give and take among yourselves. Then, there is no blame on you if you not write it down. Call witnesses when you have a transaction. Let neither one who is a scribe nor witness be pressed. If you accomplish that, then, it is, truly, disobedience on your part. So be Godfearing of God. God teaches you. God is Knowing of everything.

88. CHAPTER 8: THE SPOILS OF WAR (AL-ANFAL)

8:12 Mention when thy Lord reveals to the angels: I am, truly, with you, so <u>make</u> those who believed <u>firm</u>. I will cast alarm into the hearts of those who were ungrateful. So, (angels), <u>strike</u> above their necks and strike each of their fingers from them.

8:20 O those who believed! <u>Obey</u> God and His Messenger and turn not away from him when you hear his command.

8:24-8:26 O those who believed! <u>Respond</u> to God and to the Messenger when He called you to what gives you life. <u>Know</u>, truly, that God comes between a man and his heart and that to Him you will assemble. <u>Be Godfearing</u> of a test which will not light on those of you, particularly, who did wrong. Know that God is, truly, Severe in repayment. <u>Remember</u> when you were few, ones taken advantage of due to weakness on the earth. You fear humanity would snatch you away so He gave you refuge and confirmed you with His help and provided you with what is good so that perhaps you will give thanks.

8:28 <u>Know</u> that your wealth and your children are a test and that God, with Him is a sublime compensation.

8:35 Their formal prayer at the House had been nothing but whistling and clapping of hands. So <u>experience</u> the punishment because you had been ungrateful.

8:39 <u>Fight</u> them until there be no persecution and the way of life—all of it—be for God. Then, if they refrained themselves, then, truly, God is Seeing of what they do.

8:40 If they turned away, then, <u>know</u> that God is your Defender. How excellent a Defender and how excellent a Helper!

8:41 <u>Know</u> that whatever thing you gain as booty, then, truly one-fifth of it belongs to God and to the Messenger and to the possessors of kinship and the orphans and the needy and the traveler of the way. if you had been believing in God and in what We caused to descend to Our servant on the Day of the Criterion between right and wrong, the day when the two multitudes met one another. God is Powerful over everything.

8:45 O those who believed! When you met a faction, then, <u>stand firm</u> and <u>remember</u> God frequently so that perhaps you will prosper.

8:46 <u>Obey</u> God and His Messenger and contend not with one another. Then, you lose heart and your competence go. <u>Have patience</u>. Truly, God is with the ones who remain steadfast.

8:50 If **you** would see when those who were ungrateful are called to themselves by the angels, they are striking their faces and their backs saying: <u>Experience</u> the punishment of the burning.

8:60 <u>Prepare</u> for them whatever you were able of strength, including a string of horses, to put fear in the enemy of God and your enemy and others besides whom you know them not. God knows them. Whatever thing you spend in the way of God, the account will be paid in full to you and you will not be wronged.

8:69 Eat of what you gained as booty, lawful, what is good. <u>Be Godfearing</u> of God. Truly, God is Forgiving, Compassionate.

89. CHAPTER 3: THE FAMILY OF IMRAN (AL-I IMRAN)

3:32 Say: <u>Obey</u> God and the Messenger. Then, if they turned away, then, truly, God loves not the ones who are ungrateful.

3:61 Then, to whoever argued with **you** about it after what drew near **you** of the knowledge, say: <u>Approach</u> now! Let us call to our children and your children and our women and your women and ourselves and yourselves. Again we will humbly supplicate, and we lay the curse of God on the ones who lie.

3:81 Mention when God took a solemn promise from the Prophets: Whatever I gave you of the Book and wisdom, again, if a Messenger drew near you with that which establishes as true what is with you, you will believe in him and you will help him. He said: Are you in accord? Will you take on My severe test? They said: We are in accord. He said: Then, <u>bear witness</u> and I am with you among the ones who bear witness.

3:102 O those who believed! <u>Be Godfearing</u> of God as it is His right that He be feared. Die not but that you be ones who submit to the One God.

3:105-3:106 Be not like those who split up and are at variance after the clear portents have drawn near them. Those, for them is a tremendous punishment on a Day when faces will brighten and faces will cloud over. As for those whose faces cloud over: Disbelieve you after your belief? Then <u>experience</u> the punishment for what you had been ungrateful.

3:119 Lo, behold! You are those imbued with love for them, but they love you not. You believed in the Book, all of it. When they met you, they said: We believe. But when they went privately, they bit the tips of their fingers at you in rage. Say: <u>Die</u> in your rage. Truly God is Knowing of what is within the breasts.

3:130 O those who believed! Consume not usury—that which is doubled and redoubled—and <u>be Godfearing</u> of God so that perhaps you will prosper.

3:131 <u>Be Godfearing</u> of the fire that was prepared for the ones who are ungrateful.

3:133 <u>Compete</u> with one another for forgiveness from your Lord and for a Garden whose depth is as the heavens and the earth that was prepared for the ones who are Godfearing,

3:137 Customs passed away before you. So <u>journey</u> through the earth; then, <u>look</u> on how had been the Ultimate End of the ones who deny.

3:166-3:168 What lit on you on a day when the two multitudes met one another was with the permission of God that He might know the ones who believe and He would know those who were hypocrites. It was said to them: <u>Approach</u> now! <u>Fight</u> in the way of God or <u>drive back</u>. They said: If we would have known there would be fighting, we would, certainly, have followed you. They were nearer to disbelief on that day than to belief. They say with their mouths what is not in their hearts. God is greater in knowledge of what they keep back. Those who said to their brothers while they sat back: If they obeyed us, they would not have been slain. Say: Then, <u>drive off</u> death from yourselves, if you had been ones who are sincere.

3:175 It is only Satan who frightens you with his protectors. So fear them not, but <u>fear</u> Me if you had been ones who believe.

3:179 God had not been forsaking the ones who believe to what you are in until He differentiates the bad from what is good. God will not inform about the unseen, but God elects from His Messengers whom He wills. So <u>believe</u> in God and His Messengers. If you believe and are Godfearing, then, for you there is a sublime compensation.

3:181 Certainly, God heard the saying of those who said: Truly, God is poor and we are rich. We will write down what they said and their killing of the Prophets without right. We will say: <u>Experience</u> the punishment of the burning!

3:193 Our Lord! Truly, we heard one who calls out, cries out for belief: <u>Believe</u> in your Lord! So we believed. Our Lord! So forgive **You** our impieties and absolve us of our evil deeds and gather us to **You** with the pious.

3:200 O those who believed! <u>Excel in patience</u> and <u>be steadfast</u>. Be God-

<u>fearing</u> of God so that perhaps you will prosper.

90. Chapter 33: The Confederates (al-Ahzab)

33:5 <u>Call</u> to them by the names of their fathers. That is more equitable with God. But if you know not their fathers, they are your brothers in the way of life and your defenders. There is no blame on you in what mistake you made in it, but what your hearts premeditated. God had been Forgiving, Compassionate.

33:9 O those who believed! <u>Remember</u> the divine blessing of God to you when armies drew near you and We sent the winds against them and armies you see not. God had been Seeing of what you do.

33:13 When a section of them said: O people of Yathrib! There is no habitation for you, so <u>return</u>. A group of people ask permission of the Prophet among them saying: Truly, Our houses are exposed. But they were not exposed. They want only to run away.

33:18 Surely, God knows the ones of you who hold off and the ones who converse with their brothers saying to us: <u>Come on</u>! They approach not the battle themselves but a little.

33:33 <u>Settle down</u> (f) in your (f) houses and flaunt (f) not your (f) finery as those who flaunted their finery in the previous Age of Ignorance. <u>Perform</u> (f) the formal prayer and <u>give</u> (f) the purifying alms and <u>obey</u> (f) God and His Messenger. God only wants to cause disgrace to be put away from you—People of the House—and purify you with a purification.

33:34 <u>Remember</u> (f) what is recounted in your (f) houses of the signs of God and wisdom. Truly, God had been Subtle, Aware.

33:41-33:42 O those who believed! <u>Remember</u> God with a frequent remembrance and <u>glorify</u> Him at early morning dawn and eventide.

33:49 O those who believed! If you married the females, ones who believe, and, again, divorced them before you touch them (f), then, there is no waiting period to reckon against; so <u>make provision</u> for them (f), and <u>set</u> them (f) <u>free</u>, releasing gracefully.

33:53 O those who believed! <u>Enter</u> not the houses of the Prophet for food unless permission be given to you without being ones who look for the proper time. When you were called to enter, when you have eaten your meal, then, <u>disperse</u>, and be not one who lingers for conversation. Truly, such had been to harass the Prophet and he is ashamed to ask you to leave. But God is not ashamed before The Truth. When you asked his wives for sustenance, then, ask them (f) from behind a partition. That is purer for your hearts and their (f) hearts. It had not been for you to harass the Messenger of God nor marry you his spouses after him ever. Truly, that would have been serious with God.

33:55 There is no blame on them (f) to converse freely with their (f) fathers nor their (f) sons nor their (f) brothers, nor the sons of their (f) brothers nor the sons of their (f) sisters, nor their (f) women, nor what their (f) right hands possessed. <u>Be Godfearing</u> of God. Truly, God had been Witness over everything.

33:56 Truly, God and His angels give blessings to the Prophet. O those who believed! <u>Give</u> your <u>blessings</u> to him and <u>invoke peace</u> for him.

33:70 O those who believed! <u>Be Godfearing</u> of God and say an appropriate saying.

91. CHAPTER 60: SHE WHO IS PUT TO A TEST (AL-MUMTAHINAH)

60:10 O those who believed! When the females, ones who believe, drew near to you, ones who emigrate (f), <u>put</u> them (f) to a test. God is greater in knowledge as to their (f) belief. Then, if you knew them (f) as ones who believe (f), return them (f) not to the ones who are ungrateful. They (f) are not allowed to them (m) nor are they (m) lawful for them (f). Give them (m) what they (m) have spent. There is no blame on you that you (m) marry them (f) when you have given them (f) their compensation. Hold back conjugal ties with the ones who are ungrateful and ask for what you (m) spent and let them ask for what they (m) spent. That is the determination of God. He gives judgment among you. And God is Knowing, Wise.

60:11-60:12 If any slipped away from you of your spouses to the ones who are ungrateful, then, you retaliated and <u>give</u> the like to whose spouses went of what they (m) spent. <u>Be Godfearing</u> of God in Whom you are ones who believe. O Prophet! When drew near thee the females, ones who are believers, to take the pledge of allegiance to thee that they will ascribe nothing as partners with God nor will they steal nor will they commit adultery nor will they kill their children, nor will they approach making false charges to harm another's reputation that they devise between their (f) hands and their (f) feet, and that they rebel not against thee in anything that is honorable. Then, <u>take</u> their (f) pledge of allegiance and <u>ask forgiveness</u> from God for them (f). Truly, God is Forgiving, Compassionate.

92. CHAPTER 4: THE WOMEN (AL-NISA)

4:2-4:6 <u>Give</u> the orphans their property and take not in exchange the bad of yours for what is good of theirs. Consume not their property with your own property. Truly, this had been criminal, a hateful sin. If you feared that you will not act justly with the orphans, then, <u>marry</u> who seems good to you of the women, by twos, in threes or four. But if you feared you will not be just, then, one or what your right hands possessed. That is likelier that you not commit injustice. <u>Give</u> wives their marriage portion as a spontaneous gift. Then, truly, if they (f) were pleased to offer to you anything of it on their (f) own, <u>consume</u> it wholesomely with repose. Give not the mentally deficient your wealth that God assigned to you to maintain for them, but <u>provide</u> for them from it and clothe them. <u>Say</u> honorable sayings to them. <u>Test</u> the orphans until when they reached the age for marriage. Then if you observe them to be of right judgment, then <u>release</u> their property to them. Consume it not excessively and hastily, for they will develop. Whoever has been rich, let him have <u>restraint</u>. Whoever has been poor, then let him consume as one who is honorable. When you have released their property to them, call witnesses over them. God has sufficed as a Reckoner.

4:8 When the division is attended by those imbued with kinship and the orphans and the needy, then, provide for them from it and <u>say </u>honorable sayings to them.

4:15-4:16 Those who approach indecency among your wives, <u>call</u> to four among you <u>to bear witness</u> against them (f). Then, if they bore witness to the affair, then, <u>hold</u> them (f) <u>back</u> in their houses until death gathers them (f) to itself or God makes a way for them (f). Those two who among you approach that, then <u>penalize</u> them both. Then, if they repented and made things right, then, <u>turn aside</u> from them. Truly, God had been Accepter of Repentance, Compassionate.

4:19 O those who believed! It is not lawful for you that you inherit women unwillingly, and place not difficulties for them (f) so that you take away some of what you gave them (f), unless they approach a manifest indecency. <u>Live</u> as one who is honorable with them (f). Then, if you disliked them (f) perhaps you dislike something in which God makes much good.

4:24-4:25 Forbidden to you are the ones who are married women, but from females whom your right hands (f) possessed. This is prescribed by God for you. Were permitted to you those who were beyond these so that with your wealth you be looking as males, ones who seek wedlock, not as ones who are licentious males. For what you enjoyed of it from them (f), <u>give</u> them (f) their bridal due as their dowry portion. There is no blame on you for what you agreed on among yourselves after the duty. Truly, God had been Knowing, Wise. Whoever of you is not affluent to be able to marry the ones who are free, chaste females, the female believers, then, from females whom your right hands possessed, the ones who are female spiritual warriors, female believers God is greater in knowledge about your belief. You are of one another. So <u>marry</u> them (f) with the permission of their people, and <u>give</u> them (f) their bridal due as one who is honorable, they being ones who are free, chaste females, without being ones who are licentious females, nor females, ones who take lovers to themselves. When they (f) are in wedlock, if they (f) approached indecencies, then on them is half of the ones who are free, chaste females of the punishment. That is for those who dreaded fornication among you. It is better for you that you endure patiently. God is Forgiving, Compassionate.

4:32-4:36 Covet not what God gave as advantage of it to some of you over others. For men is a share of what they deserved and for women is a share of what they (f) deserved. <u>Ask</u> God for His grace. Truly, God had been Knowing of everything. To everyone We assigned inheritors to what the ones

who are your parents and the nearest kin left. Those with whom you made
an agreement with your sworn oaths, then, <u>give</u> them their share. Truly, God
had been Witness over everything. Men are supporters of wives because God
gave some of them an advantage over others and because they spent of their
wealth. So the females, ones in accord with morality are the females, ones
who are morally obligated and the females, ones who guard the unseen of
what God kept safe. Those females whose resistance you fear, then <u>admonish</u>
them (f) and <u>abandon</u> them (f) in their sleeping places and <u>go away</u> from
them (f). Then if they (f) obeyed you, then look not for any way against them
(f). Truly, God had been Lofty, Great. If you feared a breach between the
two, then, <u>raise up</u> an arbiter from his people and an arbiter from her people.
If they both want to make things right, God will reconcile it between the two.
Truly, God had been Knowing, Aware. Worship God and ascribe nothing as
partners with Him. (Show) kindness to the ones who are your parents and to
the possessors of kinship and the orphans and the needy, to the neighbor who
is as a possessor of strangeness and the neighbor who is kin and to the companion by your side and the traveler of the way and whom your right hands
possessed. Truly, God loves not ones who had been proud, boastful,

4:43 O those who believed! Come not near the formal prayer while you
are intoxicated until you know what you are saying nor defiled but as one
who passes through a way until you wash yourselves. If you had been sick
or on a journey or one of you drew near from the privy or you came into sexual contact with your wives and you find no water, then, <u>aim at getting</u> wholesome, dry earth. Then, wipe your faces and your hands. Truly, God had been
Pardoning, Forgiving.

4:47 O those who were given the Book! <u>Believe</u> in what We sent down,
that which establishes as true what was with you, before We obliterate faces,
and repel them backward or curse them as We cursed the Companions of the
Sabbath. The command of God had been one that is accomplished.

4:59 O those who believed! <u>Obey</u> God and <u>obey</u> the Messenger and those
imbued with authority among you. Then, if you contended with one another
in anything, refer it to God and the Messenger if you had been believing in
God and the Last Day. That is better and a fairer interpretation.

4:61 When it was said to them: <u>Approach</u> now to what God caused to
descend and approach now to the Messenger, **you** had seen the ones who are
hypocrites barring thee with hindrances.

4:66 If We prescribed for them that you: <u>Kill</u> yourselves, or: <u>Go forth</u>
from your abodes, they would not have accomplished it, but a few of them.
Had they accomplished what they are admonished by it, it would have been
better for them and a stauncher confirming.

4:71 O those who believed! <u>Take</u> your precautions. Then, <u>move forward</u>
in companies of men or <u>move forward</u> altogether.

4:76-4:77 Those who believed fight in the way of God. Those who were ungrateful fight in the way of the false deity. So <u>fight</u> the protectors of Satan. Truly the cunning of Satan had been weak. Have **you** not considered those who when it was said to them: <u>Limit</u> your hands from warfare and <u>perform</u> the formal prayer and <u>give</u> the purifying alms? Then, when fighting was prescribed for them, there was a group of people among them who dread humanity, even dreading God or with a more severe dreading, and they said: Our Lord! Why had **You** prescribed fighting for us? Why had **You** not postponed it for another near term for us? Say: The enjoyment of the present is little and the world to come is better. For whomever was Godfearing, you will not be wronged in the least.

4:86 When you were given greetings with greetings, then, <u>give greetings</u> fairer than that or <u>return</u> the same to them. Truly, God had been over everything a Reckoner.

4:89 They wished for you to be ungrateful as they were ungrateful so you become equals. So take not to yourselves protectors from them until they emigrate in the way of God. Then, if they turned away, then, <u>take</u> them and <u>kill</u> them wherever you found them. Take not to yourselves from them either a protector or a helper,

4:91 You will find others who want that they be safe from you and that they be safe from their folk. Whenever they were returned to temptation, they were overthrown in it. So if they withdraw not from you, nor give a proposal of surrender to you and limit not their hands, then, <u>take</u> them and <u>kill</u> them wherever you came upon them. Those, We made for you a clear authority against them.

4:94 O those who believed! When you traveled in the way of God, then <u>be clear</u> and say not to whomever gave you a proposal of peace: You are not one who believes, looking for advantage in this present life. With God is much gain. Thus, you had been like that before, then God showed grace to you, so <u>be clear</u>. Truly, God had been Aware of what you do.

4:103 Then, when you satisfied the formal prayer, then, remember God when upright and sitting and on your sides. Then, when you were secured, <u>perform</u> the formal prayer. Truly, the formal prayer had been—for the ones who believe—a timed prescription.

4:106 <u>Ask</u> God <u>for forgiveness</u>. Truly, God had been Forgiving, Compassionate.

4:131 To God is whatever is in the heavens and whatever is in and on the earth and, certainly, We charged those who were given the Book before you, and to you, that you <u>be Godfearing</u> of God alone. If you are ungrateful, then, truly, to God belongs whatever is in the heavens and whatever is in and on the earth. God had been Sufficient, Worthy of Praise.

4:135-4:136 O those who believed! <u>Be</u> staunch in equity as witnesses to God even against yourselves or the ones who are your parents or the nearest of kin, whether you would be rich or poor, then God is Closer to both than you are. So follow not your desires that you become unbalanced. If you distort or turn aside, then, truly, God had been Aware of what you do. O those who believed! Believe in God and His Messenger and the Book which He sent down to His Messenger and the Book that He caused to descend before. And whoever is ungrateful to God and His angels and His Books and His Messengers and the Last Day, then, surely, went astray, a wandering far astray.

4:170 O humanity! Surely, the Messenger drew near you with The Truth from your Lord. So believe, it is better for you. And if you are ungrateful, then, truly, to God is whatever is in the heavens and the earth. And God had been Knowing, Wise.

94. CHAPTER 57: IRON (AL-HADID)

57:7 Believe in God and His Messenger and spend out of what He made you ones who are successors in it. Those among you who believed and spent, for them is a great compensation.

57:13 On a Day will say the males, ones who are hypocrites and females, the ones who are hypocrites to those who believed: Wait for us that we will borrow from your light. It will be said: Return behind and search out for a light. There would be a fence set up between them for which there is a door. That which is inward is mercy and that which is outward is towards the punishment.

57:17 Know you that God gives life to the earth after its death. Surely, We made manifest the signs to you so that perhaps you will be reasonable.

57:20 Know that this present life is only a pastime, a diversion and an adornment and a mutual boasting among you and a rivalry in respect to wealth and children as the likeness of plenteous rain water. The plants impressed ones who are ungrateful. Again, it withers; then, thou hast seen it yellowing. Again, it becomes chaff while in the world to come there is severe punishment and forgiveness from God and contentment. This present life is nothing but a delusion of enjoyment.

57:21 Move quickly towards forgiveness from your Lord and the Garden whose depth is as the breadth of the heavens and earth. It was prepared for those who believed in God and His Messengers. That is the grace of God. He gives it to whom He wills. God is The Possessor of the Sublime Grace.

57:28 O those who believed! Be Godfearing of God and believe in His Messenger. He will give you a double like part of His mercy. He assigns you a light to walk by. He will forgive you. God is Forgiving, Compassionate.

95. CHAPTER 47: THE CURVING SANDHILLS (AL-AHQAF)

47:4 So when you met those who were ungrateful, then, strike their thick necks until you gave them a sound thrashing. Then, tie them fast with restraints. Afterwards either have good will towards them or take ransom for them until the war ends, laying down its heavy load. Thus, it is so! But if God willed, He Himself would have, certainly, avenged you. But it is to try some of you with some others. As for those who were slain in the way of God, He will never cause their actions to go astray.

47:33 O those who believed! <u>Obey</u> God and <u>obey</u> the Messenger and render not your actions untrue.

97. CHAPTER 55: THE MERCIFUL (AL-RAHMAN)

55:9 <u>Set up</u> the weighing with justice and skimp not in the Balance.

99. CHAPTER 65: DIVORCE (AL-TALAQ)

65:1 O Prophet! When you divorced your wives, then, <u>divorce</u> them (f) after their (f) waiting periods and <u>count</u> their (f) waiting periods. <u>Be God-fearing</u> of God, your Lord. Drive them (f) not out from their (f) houses nor let them (f) go forth unless they approach a manifest indecency. These are the ordinances of God. And whoever violates the ordinances of God, then, truly, he did wrong to himself. **You** are not informed so that perhaps God will cause to evoke something after that affair.

65:2 Then, when they (f) reached their (f) term, either <u>hold</u> them (f) <u>back</u> as one who is honorable or <u>part</u> from them (f) as one who is honorable and <u>call</u> to witnesses from two possessors of justice from among you and <u>perform</u> testimony for God. That is admonished for whomever had been believing in God and the Last Day. He who is Godfearing of God, He will make a way out for him.

65:6 <u>Cause</u> them (f) <u>to dwell</u> where you inhabited according to what you are able to afford and be not pressing them (f), putting them (f) in straits. If they (f) had been imbued with pregnancy, then, <u>spend</u> on them (f) until they bring forth their (f) burden. Then, if they (f) breast feed for you, <u>give</u> them (f) their compensation. Each of you <u>take counsel</u> between you as one who is honorable. But if you make difficulties for one another, then, another would breast feed on behalf of the father.

65:10 God prepared for them a severe punishment. So <u>be Godfearing</u> of God, O those imbued with intuition, those who believed! Surely, God caused to descend to you a Remembrance.

101. CHAPTER 59: THE BANISHMENT (AL-HASHR)

59:2 It is He Who drove out those who were ungrateful—among the People of the Book—from their abodes at the first assembling. You thought that they would not go forth. They thought that they are ones who are secure in their fortresses from God. But God approached them from where they anticipate not. He hurled alarm into their hearts. They devastate their own houses with their own hands and the hands of the ones who believe. Then, <u>take warning</u>, O those imbued with insight!

59:7 What God gave to His Messenger as spoils of war from the people of the towns is for God and His Messenger and the possessors of kinship and the orphans and the needy and the traveler of the way so that it be changing not hands between the rich among you. Whatever the Messenger gave you, take it. Refrain yourselves from what he prohibited you. Be Godfearing of God. Truly, God is Severe in repayment.

59:9 Those who took their abodes as dwellings and had belief before them, love them who emigrated to them and they find not in their breasts any need for what the emigrants were given and hold them in greater favor over themselves even though they themselves had been in destitution. Whoever is protected from his own stinginess, then, those, they are the ones who prosper.

59:18 O those who believed! Be Godfearing of God and let every soul look on what is put forward for tomorrow. Be Godfearing of God. Truly, God is Aware of what you do.

102. CHAPTER 24: THE LIGHT (AL-NUR)

24:2 The one who is an adulteress and the one who is an adulterer, scourge each one of them one hundred strokes. Let not tenderness for them take you from the judgment of God, if you had been believing in God and the Last Day. Let them bear witness to their punishment by a section of the ones who believe.

24:4 Those who accuse the ones who are free, chaste (f) and, again, bring not four witnesses, then, let them be scourged eighty strokes and never accept their testimony. Those, they are the ones who disobey.

24:28 If you find not in it anyone, then, enter them not until permission be given to you. If it was said to you: Return, then, return. It is purer for you. God is Knowing of what you do.

24:31-24:33 Say to the females, ones who believe to lower their (f) sight and keep their (f) private parts safe and show not their (f) adornment but what is manifest of it. And let them (f) draw their head coverings over their (f) bosoms; and not show their (f) adornment but to their (f) husbands or their (f) fathers or the fathers of their (f) husbands or their sons or the sons of their (f) husbands or their (f) brothers or the sons of their (f) brothers or the sons of their (f) sisters or their (f) women, or what their (f) right hands possessed, or the ones who heed, imbued with no sexual desire among the men or small male children to whom was not manifest nakedness of women. And let them (f) not stomp their feet so as to be known what they (f) conceal of their adornment. Turn to God altogether for forgiveness. O the ones who believe, so that perhaps you will prosper. Wed the single among you to the ones in accord with morality of your male bond servants and your female bond servants. If they be poor, God will enrich them of His grace. God is One Who is Extensive, Knowing. Let those who find not the means for marriage have restraint

until God enriches them of His grace. For those who are looking for eman-
cipation from among what your right hands possessed, <u>contract</u> with them if
you knew good in them. <u>Give</u> them of the wealth of God which He gave you.
Compel not your spiritual warriors (f) against their will to prostitution when
they (f) wanted chastity, that you be looking for the advantage of this present
life. And whoever compels them (f) to it against their (f) will, yet after their
(f) compulsion, God will be of them (f), the female, Forgiving, Compassionate.

24:54 Say: <u>Obey</u> God and <u>obey</u> the Messenger. But if you turn away,
then, on him was only what was loaded on him, and on you was only what
was loaded on you. If you obey him, you will be truly guided. There is not a
duty on the Messenger but the delivering of the clear message.

24:56 <u>Perform</u> the formal prayer and <u>give</u> the purifying alms and <u>obey</u>
the Messenger so that perhaps you will find mercy.

24:61 There is no fault on the blind nor fault on the lame nor fault on
the sick nor on yourselves that you eat from your houses or the houses of
your fathers or the houses of your mothers or the houses of your brothers or
the houses of your sisters or the houses of your paternal uncles or the houses
of your paternal aunts or the houses of your maternal uncles or the houses of
your maternal aunts or of that for which you possess its keys or your ardent
friend. There is no blame on you that you eat altogether or separately. But
when you entered houses, then, <u>greet</u> one another with a greeting from God,
one that is blessed and what is good. Thus, God makes manifest for you the
signs so that perhaps you will be reasonable.

24:62 The ones who believe are only those who believe in God and His
Messenger. When they had been with him on a collective matter, they go not
until they asked his permission. Truly, those who ask thy permission, those
are those who believed in God and His Messenger. So when they ask **your**
permission for some of their affairs, <u>give permission</u> to whom **you** had willed
of them, and <u>ask</u> God <u>for forgiveness</u> for them. Truly, God is Forgiving, Compassionate.

103. CHAPTER 22: THE PILGRIMAGE (AL-HAJJ)

22:1 O humanity! <u>Be Godfearing</u> of your Lord. Truly, the earthquake of
the Hour is a tremendous thing. On a Day you will see it,

22:22 Whenever they wanted to go forth from there because of lament,
they will be caused to return to it and <u>experience</u> the punishment of the burning.

22:27-22:28 Announce to humanity the pilgrimage to Makkah. They will
approach **you** on foot and on every thin camel. They will approach from
every deep ravine that they may bear witness to what profits them and remember the Name of God on known days over whatever He provided them
from flocks of animals. Then, <u>eat</u> of it and <u>feed</u> the ones who are in misery

and the poor.

22:30 That was commanded! Whoever holds the sacred things of God in honor, then, that is better for him with his Lord. Permitted to you were the flocks, but what will be recounted to you. So <u>avoid</u> the disgrace of graven images and <u>avoid</u> saying the untruth.

22:34 For every community We assigned devotional acts that they may remember the Name of God over what We provided them of flocks of animals. Your God is One God. <u>Submit</u> to Him, and give **you** good tidings to the ones who humble themselves,

22:36 We made for you the beasts of sacrifice among the waymarks of God. You have in them much good so <u>remember</u> the Name of God over them, ones who are standing in ranks. Then, when they collapsed on their sides, eat from them and feed the ones who are paupers and the ones who are poor persons who beg not. Thus, We caused them to be subservient to you so that perhaps you will give thanks.

22:73 O humanity! A parable was propounded, so <u>listen</u> to it. Truly, those whom you call to other than God will never create a fly, even if they were gathered together for it. When the fly is to rob them of something, they would never seek to deliver it from the fly. Weak were the ones who are seekers and the ones who are sought.

22:77 O those who believed! <u>Bow down</u> and <u>prostrate</u> yourselves, and <u>worship</u> your Lord, and <u>accomplish good</u> so that perhaps you will prosper.

22:78 <u>Struggle</u> for God in a true struggling. He elected you and made not for you in your way of life any impediment. It is the creed of your father Abraham. He named you the ones who submit to God before and in this Recitation that the Messenger be a witness over you and you are witnesses over humanity. So <u>perform</u> the formal prayer and <u>give</u> the purifying alms and <u>cleave</u> firmly to God. He is your Defender. How excellent a Defender and how excellent a Helper!

104. CHAPTER 63: THE HYPOCRITES (AL-MUNAFIQUN)

63:5 When it was said to them: <u>Approach</u> now. The Messenger of God asks forgiveness for you. They twist their heads and **you** had seen them dissuading while they are ones who grow arrogant.

63:10 <u>Spend</u> of what We provided you before approaches death to any of you. Then, he will say: My Lord! If only **You** would postpone it for a little term then, I would be charitable and be among the ones in accord with morality.

105. CHAPTER 58: SHE WHO DISPUTES (AL-MUJADILAH)

58:9 O those who believed! When you hold secret counsel, <u>hold</u> not secret counsel in sin and deep-seated dislike and in opposition to the Messenger. But hold secret counsel for virtuous conduct and God-consciousness and <u>be</u>

Godfearing of God before Whom you will be assembled.

58:11-58:13 O those who believed! When it was said to you: Make ample space in the assemblies, then, make room. God will make room for you. When it was said: Move up, then, move up. God will exalt those among you who believed and those who were given the knowledge in degrees. And God is Aware of what you do. O those who believed! When you consulted with the Messenger, put charity forward in advance of your conversing privately. That is better for you and purer. But if you find not the means, then, truly, God is Forgiving, Compassionate. Are you apprehensive to put forward charity in advance of your conversing privately? If, then, you accomplish it not, God turned in forgiveness to you. Perform the formal prayer and give the purifying alms and obey God and His Messenger. God is Aware of what you do.

106. CHAPTER 49: THE INNER APARTMENTS (AL-HUJURAT)

49:6-49:7 O those who believed! If one who disobeys drew near to you with a tiding, then, be clear so that you not light on a folk out of ignorance. Then, you would become ones who are remorseful for what you accomplished. Know you that the Messenger of God is of you. If he obeys you in much of the affairs, you would, certainly, fall into misfortune. But God endeared belief to you and made it appear pleasing to your hearts. He caused to be detestable to you ingratitude and disobedience and rebellion. Those, they are the ones who are on the right way.

49:9 If two sections among the ones who believe fought one against the other, then, make things right between them both. Then, if one of them was insolent against the other, then, fight the one who is insolent until it changed its mind about the command of God. Then, if it changes its mind, make things right between them justly. Act justly. Truly, God loves the ones who act justly.

49:12 O those who believed! Avoid suspicion much. Truly, some suspicion is a sin. Spy not nor backbite some by some other. Would one of you love to eat the flesh of his lifeless brother? You would have disliked it. Be Godfearing of God. Truly, God is Accepter of Repentance, Compassionate.

107. CHAPTER 66: THE FORBIDDING (AL-TAHRIM)

66:6 O those who believed! Protect yourselves and your people from a fire whose fuel is humanity and rocks over which are angels, harsh, severe who rebel not against whatever God commanded them and they accomplish what they are commanded.

66:8 O those who believed! Turn to God for forgiveness remorsefully, faithfully. Perhaps your Lord will absolve you of your evil deeds and cause you to enter into Gardens beneath which rivers run. On the Day God will not cover the Prophet with shame and those who believed with him. Their light will hasten about between them and on their right. They will say: Our Lord!

Fulfill for us our light and forgive us. Truly, **You** are Powerful over everything.

108. CHAPTER 64: THE MUTUAL LOSS AND GAIN (AL-TAGHABUN)

64:8 So believe in God and His Messenger, and in the Light which We caused to descend. God is Aware of what you do.

64:12 Obey God and obey the Messenger. Then, if you turned away, then, it is only for Our Messenger the delivering the clear message.

64:14 O those who believed! Truly, there are among your spouses and your children enemies for you, so beware of them. If you would pardon, overlook and forgive, then, truly, God is Forgiving, Compassionate.

64:16 So be Godfearing of God as much as you were able and hear and obey and spend. That is good for yourselves, and whoever is protected from his own stinginess, then, those, they are the ones who prosper.

110. CHAPTER 62: THE CONGREGATION (AL-JUMUAH)

62:9 O those who believed! When the formal prayer was proclaimed on the day of congregation, then, hasten about to the Remembrance of God and forsake trading. That is better for you if you had been knowing.

62:10 Then, when the formal prayer had ended, disperse through the earth. Look for the grace of God. Remember God frequently so that perhaps you will prosper.

112. CHAPTER 5: THE TABLE SPREAD WITH FOOD (AL-MAIDA)

5:1 O those who believed! Live up to your agreements. Flocks of animals were permitted to you, but what is now recounted to you: You are not ones who are permitted hunting while you are in pilgrim sanctity. Truly, God gives judgment how He wants.

5:2-5:4 O those who believed! Profane not the waymarks of God nor the Sacred Month nor the sacrificial gift nor the garlanded nor ones who are bound for the Sacred House looking for grace from their Lord and contentment. When you left your pilgrim sanctity, then, hunt. And let not that you detest a folk who barred you from the Masjid al-Haram drive you into exceeding the limits. Cooperate with one another in virtuous conduct and God-consciousness and cooperate not with one another in sin and deep seated dislike. Be Godfearing of God. Truly, God is Severe in repayment. Carrion was forbidden to you and blood and flesh of swine and what of it was hallowed to other than God and the one that is a strangled beast and the one that is beaten to death and the animal one fallen to its death and the animal gored to death or eaten by a beast of prey—but what you slew lawfully—and what were sacrificed to fetishes and what you partition by divining arrows. That is contrary to moral law. Today, those who were ungrateful gave up hope because of your way of life. So dread them not but dread Me. Today, I perfected your way of life for you and I fulfilled My divine blessing on you and I was well-pleased with submission to the One God for your way of life. Whoever was driven by necessity due to emptiness—not one who inclines to sin— then, truly, God is Forgiving, Compassionate. They ask **you** what was permitted to them. Say: That which is good was permitted to you and what you taught of hunting creatures, as one who teaches hunting dogs of what God taught you. So <u>eat</u> of what they seized for you and <u>remember</u> the Name of God over it and <u>be Godfearing</u> of God. Truly, God is Swift in reckoning.

5:6-5:8 O those who believed! When you stood up for the formal prayer, then, <u>wash</u> your faces and your hands up to the elbows and <u>wipe</u> your heads and your feet up to the ankles. If you had been defiled, then, <u>cleanse</u> yourselves. If you had been sick or on a journey or one of you drew near from the privy or you came into sexual contact with your wives and you find no water, then, <u>aim</u> at getting wholesome, dry earth and <u>wipe</u> your faces and hands with it. God wants not to make any impediment for you and He wants to purify you and to fulfill His divine blessing on you, so that perhaps you will give thanks. Remember the divine blessing of God on you and His solemn promise that he made as a covenant with you by it when you said: We heard and we obeyed. <u>Be Godfearing</u> of God. Truly, God is Knowing of what is in the breasts. O those who believed! <u>Be</u> staunch in equity as witnesses to God and let not that you detest a folk drive you into not dealing justly. <u>Be just</u>. That is nearer to God-consciousness. <u>Be Godfearing</u> of God. Truly, God is Aware of what you do.

5:11 O those who believed! <u>Remember</u> the divine blessing of God on you when they, a folk, were about to extend their hands against you, but He limited their hands from you. <u>Be Godfearing</u> of God. In God let the ones who believe put their trust.

5:33-5:35 The only recompense for those who war against God and His Messenger and hasten about corruption on and on the earth is that they be killed or they be crucified and their hands and their feet be cut off on opposite sides or they be expelled from the region. That for them is their degradation in the present. For them in the world to come, there is a tremendous punishment, but for those who repented before you have power over them. So <u>know</u> you that God is Forgiving, Compassionate. O those who believed! <u>Be God-fearing</u> of God and <u>look</u> for an approach to Him and <u>struggle</u> in His way so that perhaps you will prosper.

5:38 As for the one who is a male thief and the one who is a female thief, then, <u>sever</u> their hands as recompense for what they earned, an exemplary punishment from God. And God is Almighty, Wise.

5:41 O Messenger! Let them not dishearten **you**—those who compete with one another in ingratitude among those who said: We believed with their mouths while their hearts believe not. Among those who became Jews are ones who hearken to lies, ones who hearken to folk of others who approach not **you**. They tamper with the words out of context. They say: If you were given this, then, <u>take</u> it, but if you are not given this, then, <u>beware</u>! For whomever God wants to test, **you** will never have sway over him against God at all. Those are whom God wants not to purify their hearts. For them in the present is degradation. For them in the world to come is a tremendous punishment.

5:48 We caused the Book to descend to **you** with The Truth, that which establishes as true what was before it of the Book and that which preserves it. So give judgment between them by what God caused to descend. Follow not their desires that drew near **you** against The Truth. For each among you We made a divine law and an open road. If God willed, He would have made you one community to try you with what He gave you so <u>be forward</u> in good deeds. To God is your return altogether. Then, He will tell you about what you had been at variance in it.

5:57 O those who believed! Take not to yourselves those who took to themselves your way of life in mockery and as a pastime from among those who were given the Book before you and the ones who are ungrateful, as protectors. <u>Be Godfearing</u> of God if you had been ones who believe.

5:83 When they heard what was caused to descend to the Messenger, **you** have seen their eyes overflow with tears because they recognized The Truth. They say: Our Lord! We believed so <u>write</u> us <u>down</u> with the ones who bear witness.

5:88-5:90 <u>Eat</u> of what God provided you, the lawful, what is good. <u>Be Godfearing</u> of God in Whom you are ones who believe. God will not take you to task for what is idle talk in your oaths, but He will take you to task for oaths you made as an agreement. Then, its expiation is the feeding of ten needy people of the average of what you feed your own people or clothing them or letting go of a bondsperson. But whoever finds not the means, then, formal fasting for three days. That is the expiation for your oaths when you swore them. <u>Keep</u> your oaths <u>safe</u>. Thus, God makes manifest His signs to you so that perhaps you will give thanks. O those who believed! Truly, intoxicants and gambling and fetishes and divining arrows are of the disgraceful actions of Satan. Then, <u>avoid</u> them so that perhaps you will prosper.

5:92 <u>Obey</u> God and <u>obey</u> the Messenger and <u>beware</u>. Then, truly, if you turned away, then, <u>know</u> that only on Our Messenger is the delivering of Our clear message.

5:96 The game of the sea was permitted to you and the food of it as sustenance for you and for a company of travelers, but the game of dry land was forbidden to you as long as you continued in pilgrim sanctity. <u>Be Godfearing</u> of God to Whom you will be assembled.

5:98 <u>Know</u> that God is Severe in repayment and that God is Forgiving, Compassionate.

5:100 Say: Not on the same level are the bad and what is good even if the prevalence of the bad impressed **you**. So <u>be Godfearing</u> of God, O those imbued with intuition, so that perhaps you will prosper.

5:104 When it was said to them: <u>Approach</u> now to what God caused to descend and to the Messenger, they said: Enough is what we found our fathers upon. Even though their fathers had been knowing nothing nor are they truly guided?

5:108 That is likelier that they bring testimony in proper form or they fear that their oaths will be repelled after the others' oaths. So <u>be Godfearing</u> of God and <u>hear</u>. God guides not the folk, the ones who disobey.

113. CHAPTER 9: REPENTANCE (AL-TAWBAH)

9:2-9:5 <u>Roam</u> about on the earth for four months and <u>know</u> that you will not be ones who frustrate God and that God is One Who Covers with shame the ones who are ungrateful. The announcement from God and His Messenger to humanity on the day of the greater pilgrimage to Makkah is that God is free from the ones who are polytheists and so is His Messenger. Then, it will be better for you if you repented. But if you turned away, then, <u>know</u> that you are not ones who frustrate God. Give **you** tidings to those who were ungrateful of a painful punishment. But those with whom you made a contract—among the ones who are polytheists—and again, they reduce you not at all nor do they back anyone against you, then, <u>fulfill</u> their compact with them until their term of contract expires. Truly, God loves the ones who are Godfearing. When the months of pilgrim sanctity were drawn away, then, <u>kill</u> the ones who are polytheists wherever you found them and <u>take</u> them and <u>besiege</u> them and <u>sit</u> in every place of ambush. Then, if they repented and performed the formal prayer and gave the purifying alms, then, <u>let</u> them <u>go</u> their way. Truly, God is Forgiving, Compassionate.

9:7 How will there be for the ones who are polytheists a compact with God and with His Messenger but for those with whom you made a contract near the Masjid al-Haram? If they <u>go straight</u> with you, then, go straight with them. Truly, God loves the ones who are Godfearing.

9:12 But if they broke their sworn oaths after their compact and discredited your way of life, then, <u>fight</u> the leaders of ingratitude. Truly, they, their sworn oaths are nothing to them, so that perhaps they will refrain themselves.

9:14 <u>Fight</u> them! God will punish them by your hands and cover them with shame and help you against them. He will heal the breasts of a folk, ones who believe.

9:24 Say: If had been your fathers and your children and your brothers/sisters and your spouses and your kinspeople and the wealth you gained and the transactions you dread slacken and the dwellings with which you are well-pleased were more beloved to you than God and His Messenger and struggling in His Way, then, <u>await</u> until God brings His command. God guides not the folk, ones who disobey.

9:29 <u>Fight</u> those who believe not in God nor the Last Day nor forbid what God and His Messenger forbade nor practice the way of life of The Truth among those who were given the Book until they give the tribute out of hand and they be ones who comply.

9:34-9:36 O those who have believed! Truly, there are many of the learned Jewish scholars and monks who consume the wealth of humanity in falsehood and bar from the way of God and those who treasure up gold and silver and spend it not in the way of God. Give to them tidings of a painful punishment on a Day it will be hot in the fire of hell. Then, by it are branded their foreheads and their sides and their backs. It will be said: This is what you treasured up for yourselves so <u>experience</u> what you had been treasuring up. Truly, the period of months with God is twelve lunar months in the Book of God. On the day when He created the heavens and the earth of them. Four are sanctified. That is the truth-loving way of life. So do not wrong yourselves in it. <u>Fight</u> the ones who are polytheists collectively, as they fight you collectively. <u>Know</u> that God is with the ones who are Godfearing.

9:38 O those who believed! What was it with you when was said to you: <u>Move forward i</u>n the way of God, you inclined heavily downwards to the earth? Were you so well-pleased with this present life instead of the world to come? But the enjoyment of this present life is not but little compared to the world to come.

9:41 <u>Move forward</u> light and heavy and <u>struggle</u> with your wealth and your lives in the way of God. That is better for you if you had been knowing.

9:46 If they wanted to go forth, certainly, they would have prepared for it some preparation, except God disliked arousing them, so He caused them to pause and it was said: <u>Sit</u> along with the ones who sit at home.

9:52 Say: Are you watching for something, but one of the two fairer things to befall us? We watch for you, whether God will light on you a punishment from Him or from our hands. So <u>watch</u>! We are ones who are waiting with you.

9:53 Say: <u>Spend</u> willingly or unwillingly. There will be only non-acceptance. Truly, you, you had been a folk, ones who disobey.

9:64 The ones who are hypocrites are fearful that should be sent down against them a Chapter of the Quran to tell them what is in their hearts. Say: <u>Ridicule</u> us, but, truly, God is One Who Drives Out that of which you are fearful.

9:83 Then, God returned **you** to a section of them. They asked **your** permission for going forth. Then, say: You will never ever go forth with me nor fight an enemy with me. You were well-pleased sitting the first time. Then, <u>sit</u>—ones who await with who lagged behind.

9:86 When a Chapter of the Quran was caused to descend saying that: <u>Believe</u> in God and <u>struggle</u> along with His Messenger, those imbued with affluence ask permission of thee. And they said: Forsake us. We would be with the ones who sit at home.

9:95 They will swear to you by God when you turned about to them so that you <u>renounce</u> them. So renounce them. Truly, they are a disgrace. And their place of shelter will be hell, as a recompense for what they had been earning.

9:105 Say: <u>Act</u>! God will consider your actions and so will His Messenger and the ones who believe. You will be returned to Him, One Who Knows of the unseen and the visible. Then, He will tell you what you had been doing.

9:111 Truly, God bought from the ones who believe themselves and their properties. For them is the Garden! They fight in the way of God so they kill and are slain. It is a promise rightfully on Him in the Torah and the Gospel and the Quran. Who is more true to His compact than God? Then, <u>rejoice</u> in the good tidings of the bargain that you made in trading with Him. That, it is the winning the sublime triumph

9:119 O those who believed! <u>Be Godfearing</u> of God and be with the ones who are sincere.

9:123 O those who have believed! <u>Fight</u> the ones who are close to you of the ones who are ungrateful. Let them find harshness in you. <u>Know</u> that God is with the ones who are Godfearing.

BIBLIOGRAPHY

Abou El Fadl, Khaled, "What is Sharia?" March 22, 2011.

Bakhtiar, Laleh, *The Chronological Quran as Revealed to Prophet Muhammad*. Translated and Compiled by Laleh Bakhtiar. Chicago: Library of Islam, 2015.

— *Concordance of the Sublime Quran*. Arranged by Laleh Bakhtiar. Chicago: Library of Islam, 2011.

— *The Sublime Quran: Original Arabic and English Translation*. Translated by Laleh Bakhtiar. Chicago, Library of Islam, 2007. 2 vols.

— *The Sublime Quran: English Translation*. Translated by Laleh Bakhtiar. Chicago: Library of Islam, 2007.

— *The Sublime Quran: English Translation, Pocket Size*. Translated by Laleh Bakhtiar. Chicago: Library of Islam, 2009

Shariati, Ali, *Shariati on Shariati and the Muslim Woman*. Translated by Laleh Bakhtiar. Chicago: ABC International Group, Inc. 1996.

CORRELATION OF ORIGINAL CHAPTERS
WITH CHAPTERS IN CHRONOLOGICAL ORDER

1 = 96	42 = 25	83 = 84
2 = 68	43 = 35	84 = 30
3 = 73	44 = 19	85 = 29
4 = 74	45 = 20	86 = 83
5 = 1	46 = 56	87 = 2
6 = 111	47 = 26	88 = 8
7 = 81	48 = 27	89 = 3
8 = 87	49 = 28	90 = 33
9 = 92	50 = 17	91 = 60
10 = 89	51 = 10	92 = 4
11 = 93	52 = 11	93 = 99
12 = 94	53 = 12	94 = 57
13 = 103	54 = 15	95 = 47
14 = 100	55 = 6	96 = 13
15 = 108	56 = 37	97 = 55
16 = 102	57 = 31	98 = 76
17 = 107	57 = 34	99 = 65
18 = 109	59 = 39	100 = 78
19 = 105	60 = 40	101 = 59
20 = 113	61 = 41	102 = 24
21 = 114	62 = 42	103 = 22
22 = 112	63 = 43	104 = 63
23 = 53	64 = 44	105 = 58
24 = 80	65 = 45	106 = 49
25 = 97	66 = 46	107 = 66
26 = 91	67 = 51	108 = 64
27 = 85	68 = 88	109 = 61
28 =95	69 = 18	110 = 62
29 = 106	70 = 16	111 = 48
30 = 101	71 = 71	112 = 5
31 = 75	72 = 14	113 = 9
32 = 104	73 = 21	114 = 110
33 = 77	74 = 23	
34 = 50	75 = 32	
35 = 90	76 = 52	
36 = 86	77 = 67	
37 = 54	78 = 69	
38 = 38	79 = 70	
39 = 7	80 = 78	
40 = 72	81 = 79	
41 = 36	82 = 82	

CPSIA information can be obtained
at www.ICGtesting.com
Printed in the USA
FFOW03n0758130716
25751FF